Maria Mitchell

Astronomer

Women in Science

Rachel Carson
Author/Ecologist

Dian Fossey
Primatologist

Jane Goodall
Primatologist/Naturalist

Maria Goeppert Mayer
Physicist

Barbara McClintock
Geneticist

Maria Mitchell
Astronomer

WOMEN in SCIENCE

Maria Mitchell

Astronomer

Dale Anderson

CHELSEA HOUSE
PUBLISHERS
A Haights Cross Communications Company
Philadelphia

CHELSEA HOUSE PUBLISHERS

VP, New Product Development Sally Cheney
Director of Production Kim Shinners
Creative Manager Takeshi Takahashi
Manufacturing Manager Diann Grasse

Staff for MARIA MITCHELL

Editor Patrick M. N. Stone
Production Editor Jaimie Winkler
Photo Editor Sarah Bloom
Series & Cover Designer Terry Mallon
Layout 21st Century Publishing and Communications, Inc.

A Haights Cross Communications ⌒ Company

http://www.chelseahouse.com

First Printing

1 3 5 7 9 8 6 4 2

Library of Congress Cataloging-in-Publication Data

Anderson, Dale, 1953-
    Maria Mitchell / Dale Anderson.
        p. cm.—(Women in science)
Includes index.
Summary: Profiles a Vassar professor who was one of the most famous
astronomers in the United States at the end of the nineteenth century
and whose central message to her students was "never cease to wonder."
    ISBN 0-7910-7249-5
    1. Mitchell, Maria, 1818–1889—Juvenile literature. 2. Astronomers—
United States—Biography—Juvenile literature. [1. Mitchell, Maria,
1818–1889. 2. Astronomers. 3. Scientists. 4. Women—Biography.]
I. Title. II. Women in science (Chelsea House Publishers) III. Series.
QB36.M7 A64 2002
520'.92—dc21

                                                    2002013738

Table of Contents

Introduction
Jill Sideman, Ph.D.   6

1. Watching the Sun Disappear   12

2. A Child of Nantucket: 1818–1835   20

3. Teaching and Learning: 1835–1847   28

4. Earning a Medal: 1847–1855   44

5. Expanding the Horizon: 1855–1861   54

6. Mitchell as Professor: 1862–1869   68

7. Carrying the Torch for Women: 1869–1876   80

8. The Force of Personal Character   92

   Chronology   100

   Bibliography   102

   Further Reading   103

   Index   105

Introduction

Jill Sideman, Ph.D.
President, Association for Women in Science

I am honored to introduce WOMEN IN SCIENCE, a continuing series of books about great women who pursued their interests in various scientific fields, often in the face of barriers erected by the societies in which they lived, and who have won the highest accolades for their achievements. I myself have been a scientist for well over 40 years and am at present the president of the Association for Women in Science, a national organization formed over 30 years ago to support women in choosing and advancing in scientific careers. I am actively engaged in environmental science as a vice president of a very large engineering firm that has offices all around the world. I work with many different types of scientists and engineers from all sorts of countries and cultures. I have been able to observe myself the difficulties that many girls and women face in becoming active scientists, and how they overcome those difficulties. The women scientists who are the subject of this series undoubtedly experienced both the great excitement of scientific discovery and the often blatant discrimination and discouragement offered by society in general and during their elementary, high school, and college education in particular. Many of these women grew up in the United States during the twentieth century, receiving their scientific education in American schools and colleges, and practicing their science in American universities. It is interesting to think about their lives and successes in science in the context of the general societal view of women as scientists that prevailed during their lifetimes. What barriers did they face? What factors in their lives most influenced their interest in science, the development of their analytical skills, and their determination to carry on with their scientific careers? Who were their role models and encouraged them to pursue science?

Let's start by looking briefly at the history of women as scientists in the United States. Until the end of the 1800s, not just in the United States but in European cultures as well, girls and women were expected to be interested in and especially inclined toward science. Women wrote popular science books and scientific textbooks and presented science using female characters. They attended scientific meetings and published in scientific journals.

In the early part of the twentieth century, though, the relationship of women to science in the United States began to change. The scientist was seen as cerebral, impersonal, and even competitive, and the ideal woman diverged from this image; she was expected to be docile, domestic, delicate, and unobtrusive, to focus on the home and not engage in science as a profession.

From 1940 into the 1960s, driven by World War II and the Cold War, the need for people with scientific training was high and the official U.S. view called for women to pursue science and engineering. But women's role in science was envisioned not as primary researcher, but as technical assistant, laboratory worker, or schoolteacher, and the public thought of women in the sciences as unattractive, unmarried, and thus unfulfilled. This is the prevailing public image of women in science even today.

Numerous studies have shown that for most of the twentieth century, throughout the United States, girls have been actively discouraged from taking science and mathematics courses throughout their schooling. Imagine the great mathematical physicist and 1963 Nobel Laureate Maria Goeppert Mayer being told by her high school teachers that "girls don't need math or physics," or Barbara McClintock, the winner of the 1983 Nobel Prize in Medicine and Physiology who wrote on the fundamental laws of gene and chromosome behavior, hearing comments that "girls are not suited to science"! Yet statements like these were common and are made even today. I personally have experienced discouragement of this kind, as have many of my female scientist friends.

I grew up in a small rural town in southern Tennessee and was in elementary and high school between 1944 and 1956. I vividly remember the day the principal of the high school came to talk to my eighth-grade class about the experience of high school and the subjects we would be taking. He said, "Now, you girls, you don't need to take algebra or geometry, since all the math you'll need to know will be how to balance a checkbook." I was stunned! When I told my mother, my role model and principal encourager, she was outraged. We decided right then that I would take four years of mathematics in high school, and it became my favorite subject—especially algebra and geometry.

I've mentioned my mother as my role model. She was born in 1911 in the same small Southern town and has lived there her entire life. She was always an unusual personality. A classic tomboy, she roamed the woods throughout the county, conducting her own observational wildlife studies and adopting orphaned birds, squirrels, and possums. In high school she took as many science classes as she could. She attended the University of Tennessee in Knoxville for two years, the only woman studying electrical engineering. Forced by financial problems to drop out, she returned home, married, and reared five children, of whom I'm the oldest. She remained fascinated by science, especially biology. When I was in the fourth grade, she brought an entire pig's heart to our school to demonstrate how the heart is constructed to make blood circulate; one of my classmates fainted, and even the teacher turned pale.

In later years, she adapted an electronic device for sensing the moisture on plant leaves—the Electronic Leaf, invented by my father for use in wholesale commercial nurseries—to a smaller scale and sold it all over the world as part of a home nursery system. One of the proudest days of her life was when I received my Ph.D. in physical and inorganic chemistry, specializing in quantum mechanics—there's the love of mathematics again! She encouraged and pushed me all the way through my education and scientific career. I imagine that she was just like the father of Maria Mitchell, one of the outstanding woman scientists profiled in the first season of this series. Mitchell (1818–1889) learned astronomy from her father, surveying the skies with him from the roof of their Nantucket house. She discovered a comet in 1847, for which discovery she received a medal from the King of Denmark. She went on to become the first director of Vassar College Observatory in 1865 and in this position created the earliest opportunities for women to study astronomy at a level that prepared them for professional careers. She was inspired by her father's love of the stars.

I remember hearing Jane Goodall speak in person when I was in graduate school in the early 1960s. At that time she had just returned to the United States from the research compound she established in Tanzania, where she was studying the social dynamics of chimpanzee populations. Here was a young woman, only a few years older than I, who was dramatically changing the way in which people thought about primate behavior. She was still in graduate school then—she completed her Ph.D. in 1965. Her descriptions of her research findings started me on a lifetime avocation for ethology—the study of human, animal, and even insect populations and their behaviors. She remains a role model for me today.

And I must just mention Rachel Carson, a biologist whose book *Silent Spring* first brought issues of environmental pollution to the attention of the majority of Americans. Her work fueled the passage of the National Environmental Policy Act in 1969; this was the first U.S. law aimed at restoring and protecting the environment. Rachel Carson helped create the entire field of environmental studies that has been the focus of my scientific career since the early 1970s.

Women remain a minority in scientific and technological fields in the United States today, especially in the "hard science" fields of physics and engineering, of whose populations women represent only 12%. This became an increasing concern during the last decade of the 20th century as industries, government, and academia began to realize that the United States was falling behind in developing sufficient scientific and technical talent to meet the demand. In 1999–2000, I served on the National Commission on the Advancement of Women and Minorities in Science, Engineering, and Technology (CAWMSET); this commission was established through a 1998 congressional bill sponsored by Constance Morella, a congresswoman from Maryland. CAWMSET's purpose was to analyze the reasons why women and minorities continue to be underrepresented in science, engineering, and technology and to recommend ways to increase their participation in these fields. One of the CAWMSET findings was that girls and young women seem to lose interest in science at two particular points in their pre-college education: in middle school and in the last years of high school—points that may be especially relevant to readers of this series.

An important CAWMSET recommendation was the establishment of a national body to undertake and oversee the implementation of all CAWMSET recommendations, including those that are aimed at encouraging girls and young women to enter and stay in scientific disciplines. That national body has been established with money from eight federal agencies and both industry and academic institutions; it is named BEST (Building Engineering and Science Talent). BEST sponsored a Blue-Ribbon Panel of experts in education and science to focus on the science and technology experiences of young women and minorities in elementary, middle, and high school; the panel developed specific planned actions to help girls and young women become and remain interested in science and technology. This plan of action was presented to Congress in September of 2002. All of us women scientists fervently hope that BEST's plans will be implemented successfully.

I want to impress on all the readers of this series, too, that it is never too late to engage in science. One of my professional friends, an industrial hygienist who specializes in safety and health issues in the scientific and engineering workplace, recently told me about her grandmother. This remarkable woman, who had always wanted to study biology, finally received her bachelor's degree in that discipline several years ago—at the age of 94.

The scientists profiled in WOMEN IN SCIENCE are fascinating women who throughout their careers made real differences in scientific knowledge and the world we all live in. I hope that readers will find them as interesting and inspiring as I do.

Watching the
Sun Disappear

As the last rays of sunlight disappeared, the corona burst out
all around the sun, so intensely bright near the sun that the eye
could scarcely bear it; extending less dazzlingly bright around the
sun for the space of about half the sun's diameter, and in some
directions sending off streamers for millions of miles.
—Maria Mitchell, reporting on the Denver eclipse of 1878

The train chugged westward, bringing Maria (pronounced as
"Mariah") Mitchell and her companions to Colorado. Mitchell
was the most famous woman astronomer in the United
States—in fact, she was one of the most famous astronomers,
male or female, in the country. Just a few days short of 60 years
old, Mitchell was an active, energetic scientist and teacher.

As a child, Mitchell had caught the astronomy bug from
her father. In July of 1878, though, she was not an eager young
stargazer but a professor of astronomy at Vassar Female College,

Maria Mitchell learned all she knew about astronomy from her father and from her efforts to teach herself. Despite her lack of formal education, she became one of the most highly respected scientists of her day and was the first woman to discover a comet.

a women's college in Poughkeepsie, New York. And she was leading a team of students on a scientific expedition.

The expedition nearly ended in disaster. Mitchell, two of her students, and her sister had set out by train from the East Coast. Along the way, three other students joined the group. The travelers carried three telescopes and a chronometer—a very precise kind of clock. The chronometer was delicate, so Mitchell kept it with her. The telescopes—with the glass lenses removed and packed separately from the tubes to prevent damage—traveled in large trunks.

The train voyage went well from Boston to Pueblo, Colorado. But somewhere between Pueblo and Denver, their final destination, something went terribly wrong. They reached Denver on the Wednesday before Monday, July 29th, the date of the event they were traveling to see. But only one trunk carrying a telescope arrived—and none of the lenses did. Without their instruments, the astronomers could do nothing.

Mitchell and her students waited, worrying that the equipment would not arrive. "We haunted the telegraph-rooms, and sent imploring messages," she later wrote. "We placed ourselves at the station, and watched the trains as they tossed out their freight; we listened to every express-wagon which passed our door without stopping." (Mitchell, report on eclipse) A newspaper account relates that Mitchell "expended a small fortune in telegraphing and exhausted a large fund of patience in waiting." Two days passed in frantic worry until finally, "just as we were trying to find if a telescope could be hired or bought in Denver," the lenses arrived. (Mitchell, report on eclipse)

It was the Friday before the big event. The team had to put up tents in the field, assemble the telescopes, and test the instruments to make sure they were working properly. Although there was much to do, three days seemed plenty of time.

But their worries were not over. For a week Denver had suffered through cloudy, rainy weather. It rained again on Friday, preventing them from going out into the field. It rained once more on Saturday—even harder. And on Sunday, the rain poured down even more fiercely.

The women's spirits were low. They had just one day to get ready. Worse, they might have nothing to see if the weather did not change. Adding to their gloom was a local newspaper report that "the prospect for a clear day [Monday] is not encouraging." ("Dark Doings") The little group was undoubtedly quite depressed that Sunday. After having traveled more than halfway across the country, clouds might hide what they had come to see—a total eclipse of the sun.

Mitchell and other astronomers knew that the eclipse was coming. They knew it would happen on the afternoon of July 29. And they knew it would be seen in North America.

Many parts of country would see only a partial eclipse, in which the moon covers only part of the sun. Some areas, though, would enjoy the more spectacular total eclipse, where the moon completely masks the sun. The eclipse would be total along a curve of land that stretched from Alaska through British Columbia, Montana, Wyoming, Colorado, Oklahoma, and Texas. Mitchell and her party—like several other groups of scientists—had chosen to watch the event from the area around Denver, Colorado. The city was on train lines, and they could stay with a friend of Mitchell's. She also liked the fact that Colorado "was little subject to storms"—a consideration she might have noted with irony given the poor weather they had to endure.

Excitement about the coming eclipse had been building across the United States for months. Astronomers across the county—and around the world—looked forward to the event. "Never before have preparations so elaborate been made to observe an eclipse," a *New York Times* reporter wrote. ("The Coming Total Eclipse") The scientists were excited because an eclipse reveals more about the sun than do normal days.

Many teams of scientists went west in the days before July 29. Some brought cameras to attach to their telescopes so they could photograph the moon and sun together. Some planned to look at the different kinds of light given off by the sun during the eclipse, using this information to learn more about what chemical elements could be found inside it. Many planned to look for a hidden planet that one astronomer had said orbited the sun closer than the planet Mercury.

The government sent out five official expeditions, placing each one at a different spot. There were also many private groups, with astronomers from Chicago, St. Louis, New York, Washington, D.C., and many other places. One group planned to watch the eclipse from the top of Pike's Peak, hoping to see more since the thinner air on a mountain top is clearer. Another group included famed inventor Thomas Alva Edison. He wanted to use a new instrument he had invented to learn more about the sun's heat.

All the scientific teams in Denver—like Mitchell and her party—worried about the weather. A local reporter described the "dread uneasiness" that could be felt in the different camps that rainy Sunday. ("Denver Eclipse") Fortunately, the bad weather passed. As Mitchell later recalled, "Monday morning was clear and bright." (Mitchell, report on eclipse)

Mitchell and her ladies went to work. A friend had suggested a particular open field, saying that they would not need to ask permission of the owner to use it. Mitchell thought this strange—back east she would "certainly ask permission" if she was about to use someone else's land. But she found out that her friend had been right—things were different in Colorado. "In the far West you choose your spot of ground, you dig post-holes and you pitch tents, and you set up telescopes and inhabit the land; and then the owner of the land comes to you, and asks if he may not put up a fence for you, to keep off intruders." (Mitchell, report on eclipse) Not only was the owner helpful, but some nuns who lived nearby offered tea and fresh bread to the Mitchell team.

Mitchell graciously accepted the help—and then probably firmly but politely shooed the good sisters away. With work at hand, she wanted privacy and quiet. She had hired a man to help the party with any odd tasks they needed. On the day of the eclipse, one of his tasks was to make sure that no one came near Mitchell or her students while they worked. Despite these precautions, one man did slip through and mingle with the Vassar scientists. Fortunately, the stranger did not bother them.

Mitchell placed her party at their stations. She and two students were positioned at the three telescopes. One student watched the chronometer and counted off the seconds. This would help them track the length of time that the eclipse took.

Another member of the party had the job of observing the general changes on the Earth and in the sky during the eclipse. Mitchell's sister Phebe was charged with making sketches of the event.

Tense with excitement, they waited for the leading edge of the moon to first touch the outer edge of the sun. As it neared, Mitchell told everyone except the woman calling out the time to be quiet. But the timekeeper grew short of breath from tension and briefly stopped. Mitchell, businesslike, picked up the count until the student resumed.

The moon—turned dark because the sun was behind it— became "a black notch" as the outer rim covered a part of the sun. Each person recorded in her notebook the exact time when it took place. When they compared their times, they found them a second apart.

It took an hour for the moon to fully cover the sun. In that time, the party had "little to do," Mitchell said, "but look at the beautiful scenery and watch the slow motion of a few clouds." (Mitchell, report on eclipse) They even took time out to have their picture taken.

Eventually, the moment of totality came near. Mitchell reported what happened:

> All again took their positions. The corona, which is the "glory" seen around the sun, was visible at least thirteen minutes before totality; each of the party took a look at this, and then all was silent, only the count, on and on, of the young woman at the chronometer. . . .
>
> How still it was!
>
> As the last rays of sunlight disappeared, the corona burst out all around the sun, so intensely bright near the sun that the eye could scarcely bear it; extending less dazzlingly bright around the sun for the space of about half the sun's diameter, and in some directions sending off streamers for millions of miles. (Mitchell, report on eclipse)

Mitchell viewed her first solar eclipse with her father in 1831, and she traveled to Colorado with some of her students in 1878 to view a second. Eclipses make it possible for astronomers to view the sun's corona, as well as objects near the sun that can't be seen by the human eye in normal sunlight. One theory in the 19th century was that there was another planet in the solar system that was closer to the sun than Mercury, but this idea was later proved to be erroneous.

Totality would last 2 minutes and 40 seconds. There was much to do. Those at the telescopes had to slip in new lenses — they had used tinted glass earlier, when they were looking at the bright sun. Now that the world was darkened by the moon's shadow, they needed clear glass.

The observers trained their eyes on the sun. They looked at "the shape of the corona, its color, its seeming substance." (Mitchell, report on eclipse) They looked around the sun, hoping to see the supposed new planet. When the total eclipse ended, they made careful notations of what they had seen.

As they wrote, the stillness was broken by someone shouting "The shadow! The shadow!" To the southeast, they could see the dark shadow of the moon moving across the face of the earth. What Mitchell called "a strange orange light" shone in the north and east, casting an unreal, ghostly light on the land. (Mitchell, report on eclipse)

The eclipse of 1878 was over. But the event reveals a great deal about Maria Mitchell. She was no longer the 12-year-old who counted out the seconds when helping her father study an eclipse in 1831. Now she was a respected scientist responsible for leading a team of observers. She was well organized, carefully positioning her group's telescopes and assigning tasks. She was willing to travel nearly 2,000 miles for her science. She was resourceful—when facing the disastrous possibility that the lenses would not show up on time, she tried to find replacements.

She was a careful worker—insisting on quiet as the moment neared. When the timekeeper faltered, Mitchell stepped in to continue the count, showing that she always remained focused on her task. When the team members compared the times they had found for the moment the moon first touched the sun, they were a second apart. Mitchell—who cared deeply about precision—sounds disappointed when noting this "large difference" in her report. (Mitchell, report on eclipse)

Finally, Mitchell's report reveals two other traits of her character. She was fascinated by the fact that the universe obeyed clear, fixed mathematical laws. At the same time, she was enchanted by the universe's beauty. She enjoyed the "dignified march" of the moon's shadow on the earth. And when she wrote about the strange light that touched the land after the eclipse, she marveled like a child, wondering. "Was it really the same old earth and not another planet?" (Mitchell, report on eclipse)

Astronomy revealed the precision and beauty of the universe. That's why Maria Mitchell wanted to be a stargazer.

2

A Child of Nantucket: 1818–1835

Our want of opportunity was our opportunity—our privations were our privileges, our needs were our stimulants—we are what we are partly because we had little and wanted much, and it is hard to tell which was the more powerful factor.
—**Maria Mitchell on her childhood**

Maria Mitchell was born on the island of Nantucket, off the coast of Cape Cod, on August 1, 1818. Nantucket had poor soil, and its people depended on the sea—particularly whaling—for their living. When Mitchell was born, the island was enjoying a boom that would last several decades. To hunt whales, Nantucket captains had to sail to the cold waters near the North and South Poles. While they were away for many months at a time, many of the women ran inns or shops.

Mitchell was born on Nantucket, then a small whaling community, and lived with her large Quaker family in a house by the coast. Later, when she had become a successful professor, she returned often to her hometown to vacation and spend time with her family. Nantucket is now the home of the Maria Mitchell Association.

THE MITCHELLS AND THE QUAKERS

Mitchell was born into the strict, close-knit Quaker community of the island. Quakers—members of the Society of Friends—belonged to congregations called "monthly meetings." Friends believed that the way to gain salvation was to follow the guidance of the Inner Light, so to them the internal religious experience was what really mattered in life. They did not have ministers. At meetings for worship, any member was allowed to say what the Inner Light—the working of God within the person—led him or her to say.

Quakers considered worldly things to be distractions and tried to live a "plain life." They avoided elaborate hairdos and wore dark clothing with no decorations. They did not go to the theater or play music—not even religious hymns. They did not celebrate holidays like Christmas. They avoided frivolous pastimes like games, although children were allowed to skate and ride sleighs. They used no titles such as Sir or Madam. They avoided singling out any person above other people, so they did not praise people for their accomplishments. They also did not use the word *you*. Instead, they addressed each other as *thee* and *thou*, outmoded words for *you* that had once been used among family and friends. All Quakers were expected to live disciplined, serious lives. To make sure that they did so, the monthly meeting appointed overseers who kept their eyes on how members behaved.

Maria Mitchell lived in a large and happy family amidst Nantucket's Quakers. She was the third of William and Lydia Mitchell's ten children: Andrew, Sally, Maria, Anne, Francis Macy, William Forster, Phebe, Henry, Eliza (who died in infancy), and Eliza Katherine, known as Kate. In a biography she wrote of Maria many years later, Phebe described the family's life:

> There was everything in the home which could amuse and instruct children. The eldest daughter [Sally] was very handy at all sorts of entertaining occupations; she had a delicate sense of the artistic, and was quite skillful with her pencil. . . . The girls learned to sew and cook, just as they learned to read—as a matter of habit rather than of instruction. They learned how to make their own clothes, by making their dolls' clothes—and the dolls themselves were frequently home-made, the eldest sister painting the faces much more perfectly than those obtained at the shops. . . . There were always plenty of books, and besides those in the house there was the Atheneum Library. (Albers, 19)

The Mitchell house on Nantucket (shown here), which is still standing, has a "widow's walk" on its roof. A feature of seaside homes, these were used by women in the 18th and 19th centuries to scan the horizon for signs of their husbands' ships. Mitchell and her father, however, used it as an observatory platform, a precursor to the observatory atop the Pacific Bank.

The children were each other's constant playmates and companions. At night, they slept together in three beds, cuddling during the cold winters because the bedrooms had no heat.

The older children helped to take care of the younger ones, and all helped with the chores. Maria was especially responsible for Kate, but the other young children found it easy to persuade her to take them for walks or tell them stories. She also wrote a great many poems for them. Because Maria's father did not have a steady income, the family was forced to live modestly. Maria later recalled her early years as "an endless washing of dishes." (Albers, 17) But according to Mitchell's friend and biographer Julia Ward Howe, "The drudgery necessarily entailed by narrow circumstances, was however relieved and rendered endurable by the atmosphere of thought and intelligence which gave its tone to the house." (Albers, 17)

Mitchell did indeed live in an intellectually rich environment. She could visit her relative Walter Folger, who—like his famous cousin Benjamin Franklin—was very interested in science. He was an expert clockmaker, an inventor, a student of mathematics and astronomy, a lawyer, and president of the Nantucket Philosophical Institute for a number of years as well, as state senator, congressman, and judge. She was also influenced by Phoebe Folger, a mathematician who taught her husband navigation. He later became a sea captain.

Maria's home was also full of learning. Her mother, Lydia Mitchell, worked hard to care for her large family and had little time for relaxation. She was a serious woman—so serious that Kate later said that she'd never heard her mother laugh. Nonetheless, Mrs. Mitchell found the time to pass on to her children her own great love of reading, including not only religious books but also stories and poems. Before her marriage, she had worked as a librarian, working at one library until she finished reading all the books it had and then moving to another.

MITCHELL'S RELATIONSHIP WITH HER FATHER

Maria's father, William Mitchell, was a good-humored, self-taught man. Prevented from attending Harvard College by the War of 1812, he worked, he once said, as "a cooper and soap broiler, an oil and candle manufacturer, a farmer, a schoolmaster, an insurance broker, a surveyor, a chronograph rater, an astronomical observer for the Coast Survey . . . and cashier of [the Pacific] bank." (Albers, 10) In 1837, he began earning a regular income when he was named cashier of that bank, a position he held for 24 years. Before that, though, he had taught himself mathematics and astronomy so he could make some money calculating latitudes and longitudes for the U.S. Coast Survey and rating the chronometers of whaling ships. Chronometers are delicate instruments and can lose their accuracy during an ocean voyage; by rating them, Mitchell reset them so they could work precisely again. According to son Henry, Mitchell "came in time to be the rater of all the chronometers of a fleet of ninety-two whale ships." (Albers, 13)

In this busy home, Maria Mitchell grew up. She attended various private and public schools on the island, including her father's. Mr. Mitchell would take his pupils on nature walks and tell them "thee must watch closely; then will thee see and know for thyself." (Wright, 8) On these outings, she collected shells, seaweed, flowers, and stones, a habit she kept as she got older. The last school she attended was run by the Reverend Cyrus Peirce, who would one day become director of the first teachers's college in the United States. Peirce recognized her talent in mathematics and eventually made her his assistant at the school.

But Maria's studies continued beyond the classroom on her own and with her father. It was from him that she first learned to love astronomy.

THE UNITED STATES COAST SURVEY

The Coast Survey was founded by President Thomas Jefferson in 1807 for the purpose of charting the coasts of the United States. The goal was to provide mariners with information about areas of deep water, shallows, and other conditions that affect navigation. Its first director, Ferdinand Rudolph Hassler, struggled to carry out his work as he received little funding from the government. Starting in 1832, Congress began to provide more money.

William Mitchell worked for the Coast Survey under its second director, Alexander Dallas Bache. Bache organized studies of the waters along the Atlantic and Gulf coasts. He enlisted talented scientists and officers of the Navy and the Army. He gave each person the scientific instruments needed to carry out the work. He also had people study the depth of the oceans and the animals that lived in them.

The William Mitchell schoolhouse, where Maria Mitchell's father taught celestial navigation. Her own enthusiasm for education began at an early age: in 1835, at the age of 17, she opened her own school, where she taught children aged 6 years and older a wide variety of subjects, including math, reading, and the astronomy she'd learned from her father. Later in life, at Vassar College, Mitchell would become a leader in establishing educational opportunities for women.

For William Mitchell, astronomy was more than a hobby—it was a passion. Like most homes on Nantucket, the Mitchell house had a "widow's walk"—a platform built on the roof that families used to scan the sea for the sails of their loved one's ships returning home. Mitchell used his walk as his observatory. Each night—as long as the weather was clear—he and Maria would set up their instruments, notebooks, and lamp and observe the stars and planets. Neither wind nor extreme cold stopped them. Some nights they had to first sweep the snow off the platform before they could sweep the skies with their telescope. After he went to work for the Pacific Bank and the family went to live in that building, Mr. Mitchell set up a new observatory on its roof. He also built two additional structures behind the bank, which he used to measure the movement of planets or stars across a given longitude.

Mitchell was not only devoted to astronomy—he was quite accomplished. He wrote articles for *The American Journal of Science* and received honorary master's degrees from Brown and Harvard Colleges. Through this work, he came to know many important scientists of his day.

Maria and her father became lifelong partners in astronomy. She began helping him when she was quite young. Sometimes they watched the heavens purely for enjoyment, but much of the time they were doing science. When she was just twelve and a half, she helped her father observe the solar eclipse of February 1831 by reading the chronometer. This was important work. The chronometer showed the precise time of the eclipse, which could be used to pinpoint the longitude of the house. That location had to be exact for Mr. Mitchell to accurately rate the whale captains' chronometers.

Maria's knowledge of astronomy and navigation increased over the years. When she was 14, a ship's captain came to the Mitchell home to have his chronometer rated. Since her father was away, Maria offered to do the work. The captain was skeptical but agreed to let her try since no one else was available. She did the work perfectly. Over time, she came to be widely respected on Nantucket for her abilities. She taught a number younger local men skills that a ship's officer had to have, such as how to make observations and to calculate location and time. Her brother Henry later said that she was invited to set up a navigation school but turned down the offer.

3

Teaching and Learning: 1835–1847

I saw the stars in the evening of the 10th and met them like old friends from whom I had been long parted. They had been absent from my eyes three weeks. I swept round for comets about an hour and then I amused myself with noticing the varieties of color.
—Maria Mitchell, diary entry, February 12, 1855

When she was 17 years old, Mitchell began to support herself; she continued to live on her own income until her death at the age of 70. While this is an impressive record of work—particularly for a woman who lived in the 19th century—the beginning was a modest one. She placed an advertisement in the newspaper on August 15, 1835, announcing the opening of a new school (Albers, 15):

In the 1850s, Mitchell was still learning the tricks of using a telescope, such as how to use spider silk to form makeshift crosshairs. Her interest in the stars extended beyond their scientific value; always a seeker of truth, she loved the skies for what they said to her spirit.

SCHOOL

MARIA MITCHELL proposes to open a school for Girls, on the 1st of next month, at the Franklin school house.

Instruction will be given in Reading, Writing, Spelling, Geography, Grammar, History, Natural Philosophy [science], Arithmetic, Geometry and Algebra.

Terms, $3 per quarter.
None admitted under six years of age.

Mitchell's school accepted children of all backgrounds. She had mostly white students, some black ones, and three Portuguese children who were not allowed to attend the free school in town. Some students came from families who could afford the entire tuition from the start. Others came from families who could only pay a penny at a time. Like her father, Mitchell taught her pupils to observe. She took them out at night to watch the stars and before dawn to see the world come alive. She taught them the latest scientific theories about the origin of the solar system.

A year later, Mitchell was offered the position of librarian at the Nantucket Atheneum. She left teaching and took the job, where she remained for many years. During those years, Mitchell worked very hard. In her diary she wrote, "If I should make out a calendar by my feelings of fatigue, I should say there were six Saturdays in the week and one Sunday." (Albers, 43)

In fact, Mitchell kept a relentless schedule. Her diary entry for one day reads:

> I was up before six—I made the fire in the cellar and made coffee. Then I set the table in the dining room and made a fire there. Toasted bread and trimmed lamps. At seven I rang the breakfast bell. After breakfast I made my bed and partially swept the chamber—"put up" the room. Then I came to the Atheneum and looked over my comet computations till noon. Before dinner [the mid-day meal] I did some tatting [making lace], and made seven button holes for Kate.
>
> I dressed for the Atheneum and then dined. Came again to the Atheneum at [1:30] and looked over another set of comet computations which took me until 4 o'clock. I was then pretty tired and rested by reading "Cosmos" [a book on astronomy].
>
> Lizzie Earle came in and I gossiped for half an hour. I went home to tea and as soon as tea [was done] made a loaf of graham bread. Then I went up to my room and read through (partly writing) two exercises in German which took me 35 [minutes]. It was stormy and I had no

After Mitchell discovered a comet in 1847, she modestly asked her father not to report her finding. He did so anyway, writing to the director of the Harvard College Observatory (pictured here circa 1891), William C. Bond. Bond recognized Mitchell's discovery as a new comet, and she was recognized as the first woman to discover one.

observing to do, so I sat down to my tatting. Lizzie Earle came in and I took a new lesson in tatting. . . . At a little after nine I went home with Lizzie and carried a letter to the Post Office. I had kept steadily at work for 16 hours when I went to bed. . . . (Albers, 49)

EARLY ASTRONOMY

Mitchell continued observing with her father at night. In winter, they bundled up in warm clothing and went up to the roof, hardly feeling the cold. Mr. Mitchell had complete confidence in his daughter's ability to do the work—in fact, he counted on her to carry on when he was away. On one occasion when Mitchell and other astronomers were to make coordinated observations of the same phenomenon, he wrote to William C. Bond, head of the Harvard Observatory: "If the day fixed for the [event] should be during my absence, my Maria . . . will insist on being my substitute, and . . . she will be a good one." (Wright, 44)

Father and daughter acquired more instruments over time. As they went about the work of the Coast Survey, they made notes about "the solar spots, meteors, and auroral clouds" they observed. In 1845, according to her brother Henry, they began to do original astronomical work. As he later wrote, "They entered upon systematic studies of nebulae and double stars, using the two telescopes side by side on the top of the Pacific Bank. Thenceforth . . . routine work gave place to exciting explorations." (Albers, 20)

For Maria, this work was not only scientifically interesting; she also appreciated the beauty of the stars. On February 19, 1853, she wrote in her diary, "I am just learning to notice the different colors of the stars, and already begin to have a new enjoyment. Betelgeuse is strikingly red, while Rigel is yellow. There is something of the same pleasure in noticing the hues that there is in looking at a collection of precious stones, or at a flower-garden in autumn." (Albers, 41)

Sometimes, though, astronomy was less poetic and more mundane. On one occasion, the crosshairs on a telescope broke, making it impossible to determine the positions of celestial bodies. Maria had to take the telescope apart and experiment with different materials to replace them. She found her own hair too coarse when seen through a lens and that of an infant nephew too curly. She also had trouble with the sealing wax she used to fix the crosshairs in place. At first, she applied too much of it. Another time she reassembled the telescope before the wax was completely dry, and the crosshairs slipped out of place. After consulting her friend George Bond at the Harvard Observatory, she learned how to use spider web lines from a cocoon to fix the telescope. It took her three weeks to solve the problem.

MITCHELL'S SELF-EDUCATION

By the time she was 17, Mitchell had mastered difficult mathematical and scientific texts. She had taught herself algebra, geometry, and trigonometry, annotating the margins of her books. One book that she studied in depth was Nathaniel Bowditch's *The New American Practical Navigator* (1802). Bowditch was a renowned mathematician and scientist at the time. Mitchell's brother Henry later described how dedicated she had to be to study this work:

> The "Navigator" . . . was the text-book of all the young men fitting to be whalers; but it was quite out of the question for any of these to comprehend the mathematics that lay hidden behind the practical formulas of navigation. Maria Mitchell, however, was not content with the latter, and undertook to reach the spirit of Bowditch's precepts. This was not an easy task in those days . . . and she was obliged to consult many different scientific books and the reports of mathematical societies before she could herself construct the astronomical tables. (Albers, 13)

At the Atheneum, Mitchell took advantage of the library available to her and provided herself with the equivalent of a college education. She studied calculus, physics, and astronomy—and taught herself Latin, German, and French so she could read some of the library's books on these subjects.

Mitchell's marginal comments on her books reveal her opinions of them, and she was a tough critic. In one section of a book by mathematician Karl Friedrich Gauss, she wrote, "I am losing my patience with Gauss on account of these frequent transformations which may be ingenious, but which are certainly troublesome." (Wright, 37) In another book, she wrote, "The whole work seems to have been made up from [the French mathematician Pierre Simon de] Laplace." (Wright, 37) In Sir George Airy's *Gravitation* (1834), she wrote, "This is clumsily done but is right." (Wright, 37) She seems not to have been intimidated by the fact that Airy was the head of the Royal Observatory in Greenwich, England.

Mitchell's interests were not limited to mathematics and science. She enjoyed both poetry and prose and commented

The Nantucket Atheneum was and remains the cultural and intellectual center of Nantucket. Mitchell took a position as its first librarian in 1836 and used its library to teach herself calculus, foreign languages, physics, and astronomy. On the left is the original building; it was destroyed by fire in 1846. When the Atheneum was rebuilt a year later (facing page), Mitchell began a crusade to restock its collection through purchases and donations.

in her diaries about the works of Shakespeare, John Milton, Sir Walter Scott, and Harriet Beecher Stowe. Her opinions about literature were as firm as her ideas about science: "I have just put down Mrs. Stowe's first volume of 'Sunny Memoirs.' . . . I prefer this to the second. . . . All the way through the second, I felt that I could have written as good a book. I give up the idea now, I could not have written so unobjectionable a book and at the same time used so much independent judgment." (Albers, 52)

The Atheneum, the cultural center of Nantucket, gave Mitchell many opportunities for intellectual development besides its ample library. The Nantucket Philosophical Society, directed

by William Mitchell, met there to discuss philosophical matters. So did the Social Reading Society, in which people talked about works by contemporary authors such as Walt Whitman, Charles Dickens, and the Brontës. The Atheneum also hosted regular Lyceum lectures by prominent people of the day, who discussed philosophical, social, and scientific questions. Among the speakers were the Transcendentalists Ralph Waldo Emerson and Henry David Thoreau; feminists Lucy Stone and Elizabeth Oakes Smith; religious leaders William Ellery Channing and Theodore Parker; scientists Louis Agassiz and John James Audubon; novelist Herman Melville; and reformer Horace Greeley. Many of these people were afterward guests of the Mitchell family, enabling Maria to talk to them in person.

THE CRITICAL CAPACITY

Maria Mitchell formed decided opinions about the speakers she heard and their writings. On October 27, 1854, she bitingly wrote in her diary: "Last night I heard Josiah Quincy Jr. [a former president of Harvard] lecture on the Mormons. . . . It would have

135,000 SETS, 270,000 VOLUMES SOLD.

UNCLE TOM'S CABIN

FOR SALE HERE.

AN EDITION FOR THE MILLION, COMPLETE IN 1 Vol., PRICE 37 1-2 CENTS.
"   "   IN GERMAN, IN 1 Vol., PRICE 50 CENTS.
"   "   IN 2 Vols,. CLOTH, 6 PLATES, PRICE $1.50.
SUPERB ILLUSTRATED EDITION, IN 1 Vol., WITH 153 ENGRAVINGS,
PRICES FROM $2.50 TO $5.00.

The Greatest Book of the Age.

Harriet Beecher Stowe's controversial *Uncle Tom's Cabin* (1852) revealed many of the horrors of slavery before the Civil War. In fact, some people, including Abraham Lincoln, cited the work as a cause of the war. Mitchell, a voracious reader, read the works of Stowe and other important authors, commented on them in her diaries, and sought them in restocking the Atheneum.

made a pleasant drawing room lecture but had not the dignity desirable in a Lyceum discourse, where it is presumable something will be taught." (Albers, 49) Horace Greeley, she thought, could be short-sighted. In his talk, Greeley had complained that the Smithsonian Institution was buying books that did nothing to solve immediate social problems. Mitchell wrote thoughtfully:

> Reformers are apt to forget . . . that the world is not made up entirely of the wicked and the hungry, there are persons hungry for the food of the mind, the wants of which are as imperious as those of the body. . . .
>
> Reformers are apt to forget too, that . . . you cannot lift one man above his fellows, but you lift the race of men. Newton, Shakespeare and Milton did not directly benefit the poor and ignorant but the elevation of the whole race has been through them. (Albers, 57)

Critical as she was of other people, she was equally so of herself. On October 17, 1854, after years of successful astronomical work and of having an established reputation, she wrote, "I have just gone over my comet computation again and it is humiliating to perceive how very little more I know than I did 7 years ago when I first did this kind of work." (Albers, 46) A few days earlier, she had confessed to her diary, "The best that can be said of my life so far, is, that it has been industrious and the best that can be said of me, is, that I have not pretended to what I was not." (Albers, 45) The only strength she claimed for herself was strength of will: "I was born of only ordinary capacity, but of extraordinary persistency," she wrote. (Wright, 25)

Mitchell had a sense of the absurd and was amused by the way she and other scientists were treated with great consideration and sought after at scientific meetings, only to be treated like ordinary folks as soon as they moved away from scientific circles. Tongue in cheek, she described her return trip home from one such meeting: "The descent into commoner was rather sudden. . . . [W]hen I reached out my free pass, the conductor read it through and handed it back, saying in a gruff voice, 'It's worth nothing; a dollar and a quarter to Boston.' Think what a downfall!" (Wright, 69) She also loved to hear and tell a good joke. Years after she left the island she told the story of "an old Quaker [who] rebuked a sailor, 'Friend Charles, if thee'd ever been one half as economical of this world's goods as thee is of the truth, thee'd be the richest man in Nantucket.'" (Wright, 86)

Mitchell was unconventional. Although frowned upon by strict Quakers, she began learning to play the card game whist to pass the time during the winter freeze of 1857, when neither people nor supplies could reach or leave the island. According to one account, a friend once found her sitting on the curb by a busy Boston street. When asked why she had stopped in the midst of the people and bustle of traffic, Mitchell replied simply that she was tired.

The trait for which she was most loved was her generosity. It was a valuable quality since she was honest to a fault. At the Atheneum, Mitchell befriended and mentored many of the young people of the island. One resident recalled how "Maria Mitchell always had a few moments to chat with her, questioning her about the book brought back, and noting what she had chosen for the next reading." (Wright, 87) Maria's sister Phebe wrote of how the "young girls made her their confidante and went to her for sympathy and advice. The boys, as they grew up and went away to sea, always remembered her and made a point when they returned of coming to tell their experiences to such a sympathetic listener." (Wright, 87) Mitchell greatly enjoyed these visits and took pride in their accomplishments. On April 18, 1855, she wrote in her diary: "A young sailor boy came to see me today. It pleases me to have these lads seek me on their return from their first voyage and tell me how much they have learned about navigation. They always say with pride 'I can take a lunar [measure the position of the moon], Miss Mitchell, and work it up!'" (Albers, 59)

MITCHELL LEAVES THE QUAKERS

Mitchell's thoughtful nature and independence eventually led her to leave the Quaker faith. Although she was deeply religious, Mitchell could not unquestioningly accept orthodox Quakerism.

She could accept important principles such as pacifism and the simple life. Other ideas—like the ban on music—seemed excessive, however. Precisely because religion for her involved inner understanding and experience rather than outward show, Mitchell decided to withdraw from the Nantucket meeting. Another factor might have been the fact that her older brother Andrew had been disowned by the Quakers for marrying a non-Quaker. Whatever the causes, the minutes of the women's meeting of September 28, 1843, state: "Maria Mitchell informed us that her mind was not settled on religious subjects

MITCHELL'S POETIC SIDE

Maria Mitchell had a tremendous love of poetry. She very much enjoyed Shakespeare and wanted to read Milton with an eye to his interpretation of the astronomical knowledge of his day. She was particularly well-versed in Romantic poetry, and she read the German Friedrich von Schiller's works in his native language. She liked Coleridge's "Rime of the Ancient Mariner" (1798) very much and found in Wordsworth "points of great beauty, and lines which once in the mind will not leave it."

This love of poetry influenced her travels. Her visit to Abbotsford, Sir Walter Scott's home, was one of the highlights of her trip to Europe in 1857. When she sat in his chair, she wrote, "I almost felt his presence." (Albers, 97) Mitchell also liked to have poets help her interpret the visual arts. Guided by Scott, she visited the ruins of Melrose Abbey by moonlight. At the Vatican, she read Lord Byron's description of a famous statue while standing in front of the sculpture. "A poet," she wrote, "seems to have a keener perception of the characteristic charm" and helped her "to a sense of the beauties of nature and art." (Albers, 117)

One of the oldest Quaker meetinghouses on Nantucket. Maria Mitchell grew up in a Quaker family, but she later left her meeting and became a Unitarian, a minority at the time. Although her peers sometimes thought she was not a very religious person, Mitchell was actually quite religious; Unitarianism suited her belief that reason and moral conscience should guide human life. Her scientific attitude extended to her faith.

and that she had no wish to retain her right of membership." (Albers, 22) She then attended the Unitarian Church. Over time, her four sisters and their brother Forster were also disowned by the Friends.

Conflict with Quakers touched her parents as well. The 19th century was a time of great upheaval for Quakers. Divisions arose among them over questions of doctrine and practice, such as the role of the Inner Light, the interpretation of the Bible, and the nature of Jesus Christ. Some meetings began to allow the singing of hymns. There were also social aspects to the controversy. By and large, all Friends frowned upon slavery, but some wanted to become more involved in the abolitionist movement that was working to end slavery and others did not. The controversy reached Nantucket, where the Friends divided themselves into two monthly meetings. William Mitchell and his brother Peleg found themselves in opposite groups.

As for Maria, her religious beliefs continued to develop during the following years. She lived in a time when many religious leaders objected to new scientific theories, such as Darwin's theory of evolution. She herself had no trouble reconciling science with God. She was bothered by preachers who denied the value of science and feared the work of Charles Darwin and others. In her diary, she exclaimed, "Can the study of truth do harm? Does not every true scientist seek only to know the truth? And in our deep ignorance of what is truth, shall we dread the searching after it?" (Albers, 287) She continued, "I am hopeful that scientific investigation pushed on and on, will reveal new ways in which God works and bring to us deeper revelations of the wholly unknown." (Albers, 287) For Mitchell, the Bible was not the only way that God revealed Himself. For her, "the Book of Nature is also the Book of God." (Wright, 119)

Indeed, to Mitchell, the study of nature and science would promote a deeper sense of humanity and greater spirituality:

> There will come with the greater love of science greater love to one another. Living more nearly to Nature is living farther from the world and from its follies, but nearer to the world's people; it is to be of them, with them, and for them, and especially for their improvement. We cannot see how impartially Nature gives of her riches to all, without loving all, and helping all; and if we cannot learn through Nature's laws the certainty of spiritual truths, we can at least learn to promote spiritual growth while we are together, and live in a trusting hope of a greater growth in the future. (Merriam, 96)

Regardless of the religious upheaval around them and in spite of geographic distances that later separated them, the members of the Mitchell family maintained strong ties. They corresponded with one another throughout their lives.

By 1857, all the children except Maria had married. Andrew went to sea at an early age and captained a ship during the Civil War. Sally and Anne remained on Nantucket. Francis, called Frank, stayed on Nantucket for some time but eventually moved his family to Chicago. William Forster, called by his middle name, went to Tennessee during the Civil War to work as a teacher among the newly emancipated slaves. His experiences convinced him of the evils of war and led him to become a Quaker missionary—in spite of having been disowned earlier by the Quakers for his marriage. Phebe, who was very close to Maria, ran a school of drawing and painting. After she married, she moved with her teacher husband to various places before settling in Cambridge, Massachusetts, where he was principal of a boys' school. Henry had great mathematical and scientific abilities and became a professor of hydrography at the Massachusetts Institute of Technology, studying rivers and harbors. He studied many of the major harbors along the eastern and southern coasts of the United States and performed similar work in Nicaragua and at the Suez Canal. Kate was a religious nonconformist and also very close to Maria. She married a very strict Quaker and reared her children in a traditional way.

Maria Mitchell was also extremely fond of her nieces and nephews. She loved going sea bathing with Henry's daughter Polly and then cooking a picnic over burning driftwood. She would sit with Kate's children and entertain them with fairy tales, stories, and poems. On some special occasions, she wrote poems just for them. Her niece Elma Dame remembered fondly, "I can see us now, seated on Aunt Maria's lap in my Father's big armchair, one of us on each knee, while she delighted us with children's stories and poems, read in a whimsical voice that was all her own—a voice that was adapting itself lovingly to children's ears and understanding." (Wright, 217) She also helped them with math when needed—such as the time Sally's son Mitchell was preparing for an algebra exam.

THE GREAT FIRE OF 1846

Those warm family memories were still in the future, though. In July of 1846, tragedy struck Nantucket. A great fire destroyed most of the center of the town. Over 300 buildings burned down, including the Atheneum.

The townspeople went about rebuilding as quickly as possible. As librarian, Maria was in charge of restocking the library. She set out to buy thought-provoking and informative books. From these books, she said, "the ignorant . . . perceive that a higher cultivation than theirs is in the world and they are stimulated to strive after greater excellence. So I steadily advocate in purchasing books for the Atheneum, the *lifting* of the people." (Albers, 57) Besides historical and scientific works, Mitchell purchased books like *Moby-Dick*, *Uncle Tom's Cabin*, and *The Narrative of Arthur Gordon Pym of Nantucket*. She stayed away from books that had she felt had no cultural or social value: "I despise a gossipy book of travels and I almost despise a book like 'Roughing it in the Bush' which any one could write, who had been through the scenery and out of which only amusement is obtained." (Albers, 57)

Although the fire spared the Pacific Bank building and the two smaller astronomical buildings behind it, the roof observatory was burned and some of the instruments were damaged. Worse, the astronomical records kept there were lost. So Maria and Mr. Mitchell had to rebuild their observatory and start over again.

4

Earning a Medal: 1847–1855

We congratulate the indefatigable comet seeker most heartily on her success; is she not the first lady who has ever discovered a comet?
—**Alexander Dallas Bache, letter to the Mitchell family**

COMET SIGHTED

On October 1, 1847, while sweeping the sky from the roof of the Pacific Bank building, Maria Mitchell discovered a comet. The discovery was quite significant, especially because it would have been nearly impossible for anyone less observant. Comets and other celestial objects often look very similar through small telescopes like the one that Mitchell was using. To identify the object as a comet, it was necessary to track its movement through the sky. But detailed sky charts were not available in her day to help trace the path of the comet. Her ability to identify a new comet through a small telescope

44

Comets, such as Hale-Bopp (pictured here), are basically balls of ice and cosmic dirt. They orbit the sun in ellipses, or ovals, and this typically causes them to pass by planets from time to time. Mitchell discovered a comet of her own, one that is now named after her, in 1847. The first woman ever to do so, she was awarded a gold medal from the King of Denmark for her accomplishment.

is a testament to her powers of observation and to her deep knowledge of the sky.

When Maria called her father to look at the object, he immediately agreed that it was a comet. In his diary that night, he wrote, "This evening at half past ten Maria discovered a telescopic comet five degrees above Polaris. Persuaded that no nebulae could occupy that position unnoticed [by others earlier] it scarcely needed the evidence of motion to give it the character of a comet." (Albers, 24) The modest Maria tried to persuade her father not to make a public announcement until they could provide more extensive proof. Despite that plea, Mitchell reported her find to his friend William C. Bond, the director of the Harvard College Observatory, when the next mail ship left Nantucket on October 3:

> I write now merely to say that Maria discovered a tele-scopic comet at half-past ten on the evening of the first instant [this month], at that hour nearly vertical above Polaris five degrees. Last evening it had advanced west-wardly; this evening still further, and nearing the pole. . . . Maria has obtained its right ascension and declination.
> . . . Pray tell me if it is one of George's; if not whether it was [sic] been seen by anybody. (Albers, 26)

("George" was George P. Bond, the son of the observatory's director and also his assistant.)

American scientists were thrilled by the news of Mitchell's discovery, and many people sent her congratulatory letters. Alexander Dallas Bache, the head of the U.S. Coast Survey, wrote: "We congratulate the indefatigable comet seeker most heartily on her success; is she not the first lady who has ever discovered a comet? The Coast Service is proud of her connection with it!" (Albers, 27) George Bond wrote kiddingly that she should not find any more comets until they were "announced by the proper authorities." He went on to say, ruefully, that the night before her discovery "I was sweeping within a few degrees of your prize" but had not seen the comet. (Albers, 27)

American scientists also decided to push Maria's claim to a gold medal. In 1831, the King of Denmark had promised to give such a medal to any person who discovered a comet by means of a telescope. The rules of the contest said that the discoverer had to report the comet to the Astronomer

The Pacific Bank, seen from a distance. Mitchell and her father set up their telescopes atop this building to study the stars together, and while she worked at the Atheneum Mitchell spent most of her evenings at this observatory. She adored her father and gained all her early education about astronomy and navigation from him.

Royal of Great Britain or to the observatory in Altona, Denmark, by the "next post." Mitchell's comet was not seen in Europe until October 3rd, so she was clearly the first to identify it, but she had not immediately reported it— whereas the European astronomers who had seen it had done so. In the past, other American astronomers, including George Bond, had been denied the medal because they had not met the notification requirement.

The Bonds had observed Maria's comet for some days before sending details about it to the Danish observatory, but their note explained that Maria had seen it first. Among Mr. Mitchell's civic and community activities was serving as an overseer of Harvard College. As a result, he knew Harvard's president, Edward Everett, who quickly became Maria's chief supporter and advocate. Everett hoped to promote American science, and one of his goals in supporting her claim was to make sure that American astronomers—from that point on— had a clear understanding of the contest's rule. But he also took a personal interest in Maria's cause and in one letter wrote, "It would be pleasant to have the Nantucket girl carry off

POSTHASTE?

Even if Mitchell had notified the Astronomer Royal directly of the discovery of her comet, it would probably have taken weeks to identify her as the comet's first discoverer. In the 19th century, a letter traveling by steamship across the Atlantic took at least two weeks for the crossing, and then it would have had to be sorted and forwarded to the Royal Observatory from the port of arrival.

Sending letters internationally was further complicated by the fact that countries had separate treaties with one another that established the cost of sending a letter in their different currencies. Postal workers had to figure out the correct charges for every letter. It was not until 1863 that postal administrators from 15 European countries and the United States first met to establish simpler, more uniform procedures. In 1874, 22 countries signed a treaty that established an agency and procedures for handling international mail. Called the Universal Postal Union since 1878, the agency is now an arm of the United Nations.

the prize from all the greybeards and observatories in Europe."
(Wright, 64)

Everett made the case that by notifying the Bonds at the
Harvard Observatory by the next post, William Mitchell had
complied with the requirements for the prize to the fullest
extent possible. In a letter to Christian Schumaker of the
Danish observatory, he documented the events:

> Miss Mitchell saw the comet at half-past ten o'clock on the
> evening of October 1st. Her father, a skillful astronomer,
> made an entry in his journal to that effect. On the third day
> of October he wrote a letter to Mr. Bond, the director of
> our observatory, announcing the discovery. This letter was
> dispatched the following day, being the first post-day after
> the discovery of the comet. . . .
>
> As the claimant is a young lady of great diffidence,
> the place a retired island, remote from all the high-roads
> of communication; as the conditions [of the contest]
> have not been well understood in this country; and
> especially as there was a substantial compliance with
> them—I hope His Majesty may think Miss Maria
> Mitchell entitled to the medal. (Albers, 30)

Everett's efforts were successful. In November of 1848, news
arrived from Denmark that Maria had been awarded the prize
by the King. The medal itself was sent to Everett at Harvard in
March of 1849, and he delivered it to Maria. It was made of gold,
with her name around the edge. On one side was a Latin inscription meaning "Not in vain do we watch the setting and rising of the
stars," the date of her discovery, and the words *Cometa Vistus,* or
"comet sighted." On the other side was the inscription *Christianus
Rex Daniae* (Latin for "the Christian king of Denmark").

Maria's discovery and gold medal opened many scientific
doors for her. Articles were written about her, and the Smithsonian Institution sent her a $100 prize. In 1848, she was made
an honorary member of the American Academy of Arts and

Sciences. Two years later, she became a member of the American Association for the Advancement of Science. Membership in scientific organizations enabled her to attend meetings, where she could meet with and learn from other scientists and mathematicians. Over the years, as her achievements increased and her career developed, Mitchell was awarded many other honors. She was elected to the American Philosophical Society in 1869. She received an honorary Ph.D. from Rutgers Female College in 1870 and an honorary LL.D. from Columbia University in 1887.

PROFESSIONAL SUCCESS

In 1849, the year after she received her medal, Mitchell was invited by Charles Henry Davis, superintendent of the newly created *American Ephemeris and Nautical Almanac,* to become a computer for the *Almanac.* Compiling an ephemeris—a book that provides tables showing the positions of heavenly bodies during an entire year, information that is vital to navigators—requires many long, precise, detailed calculations which today are performed by computers but in Mitchell's day were carried out by humans. Maria accepted and was assigned the calculations for the planet Venus.

That same year, A.D. Bache invited Mitchell to do her own work for the Coast Survey. The invitation was to do field work and learn from Bache himself:

> I will be glad to have Miss Maria Mitchell as an Assistant at my next station near Portland. . . . It shall be no expense to her and I will instruct and give her practice in the use of these instruments if she is willing to come. My wife is with me and we will consider Miss M. as part of my family. . . . I will also make such compensation as we make to learners. (Albers, 32)

Several years later, Mitchell expressed her gratitude for Bache's teaching: "The training of the survey is rigidly exact, and those who . . . come under Mr. Bache's immediate instruction, bear grateful testimony to the patience with which he listens to their difficulties, and to the willing ability with which he throws light upon the dark places." (Albers, 33)

Mitchell's successes did not turn her head. She continued to run the library at the Atheneum and to do astronomical work with her father. They continued to look for new comets and spotted various others, though she was never again the very first person to see one. The work sometimes involved what Maria called "a host of little annoyances" (Albers, 33), such as a moon so bright that it was hard to see other celestial bodies nearby or a broken screw that made it impossible to mount the telescope. But overall, the work continued to be a great pleasure:

> One gets attached . . . to certain midnight apparitions. The aurora is always a pleasant companion, a meteor seems to come like a messenger from departed spirits and even the blossoming of the trees in the moonlight becomes a sight looked for with pleasure. And from astronomy there is the same enjoyment . . . as in the midst of other grand scenery. There is the same subdued quiet and grateful sensuousness—a calm to the troubled spirit and a hope to the desponding. (Albers, 34)

Maria and her father became increasingly involved in the study of binary or double stars. These are pairs of stars that revolve around a point that acts as their center of gravity. This was an exciting new field of astronomy that led to important findings about the composition and evolution of stars, and many prominent astronomers of the day were engaged in the work. The Mitchells pursued the study of binary stars for many years. In 1863, Maria published an article entitled "Observations on Some of the Double Stars" in *The American Journal of Science and Arts.*

Home life and personal interests also kept Mitchell busy. She continued to read extensively and, in the 1850s, began to

Mitchell met a number of prominent figures during her visit to Washington, D.C., including Dorothea Dix, who was a staunch advocate of prison reform and care for the mentally ill. Mitchell admired Dix's optimism and quiet persistence, but Dix also inspired her to question the sacrifice of personal relationships to "do good."

develop a feminist consciousness. She attended the theater in Boston whenever possible and also visited Providence, New York, and Washington. On these trips, she got together with old friends and mingled with society people and intellectuals. In Washington, she saw A.D. Bache and met the reformer

Dorothea Dix. Typically thoughtful, Mitchell wrote the following about Dix in her diary:

> I asked her if she did not become at times weary and discouraged; and she said, wearied, but not discouraged for she had met with nothing but success. There is evidently a strong will which carries all before it, not like the sweep of the hurricane, but like the slow, steady, and powerful march of the molten lava.
>
> It is sad to see a woman sacrificing the ties of the affections even to do good. I have no doubt Miss Dix does much good, but a woman needs a home and the love of other women at least, if she lives without that of man. (Albers, 42)

Mitchell followed this advice in her own life. Although she never married, she always maintained close personal ties to her family and friends.

5

Expanding the Horizon: 1855–1861

She smiled blissfully in Rome, as if really visiting a constellation; flashing her eyes with silent laughter, and curling her soft, full splendid lips with fascinating expressions of satisfaction.
—Rosa Hawthorne, on Maria Mitchell's travels in Europe

By the mid-1850s, Mitchell wanted to expand her horizons farther. She saved money from her two jobs so she could take an extended trip to Europe. In the fall of 1856, she resigned from her position at the Atheneum and requested a leave of absence from the *Nautical Almanac*. Initially, the Secretary of the Navy would not grant her a leave, but a compromise was reached, and Maria was able to go as long as she continued preparing the computations. So Mitchell took her computation work with her on her travels.

Always searching for ways to expand her experience and her mind, Mitchell began in 1857 a lengthy voyage through the United States and Europe. Already a respected scientist by this time, she was able to meet many prominent scientists and visit a number of observatories during her travels.

THE STATES

In March of 1857, Mitchell set off for Chicago by stagecoach and train to join Prudence Swift, whose governess she was to be during a long tour. Mitchell's travel diaries are filled with acute observations of the places she saw and the people she met. One of those observations reflected changes in the general age of the population as she traveled from the eastern United States to the west: "One peculiarity in travelling from East to West is, that you lose the old men. In the cars in New England you see white-headed men, and I kept one in the train up to New York and one of grayish-tinted hair as far as Erie; but after Cleveland, no man was over forty years old." (Albers, 74)

In Chicago, she was received by "Prudie" and her banker father, H.K. Swift. Mitchell's reputation preceded her, and this notice appeared in the newspaper *The Democratic Press*:

> A Distinguished Visitor—Miss Maria Mitchell of Nantucket has been spending several days in Chicago as the guest of Gen. H.K. Swift. Most of our readers will remember that Miss Mitchell is confessedly the most distinguished lady mathematician and astronomer in the U.S., and probably among the fair cultivators of the higher mathematics she has no equal in the world of science. (Albers, 73)

Prudie's father accompanied the two women on the first leg of the trip, by steamboat down the Mississippi. Mitchell enjoyed the boat ride: "I who had been used only to the rough waters of the Atlantic coast was surprised at the little jar and the steady gliding motion of the boat. . . . I thought it the very perfection of travelling and wished all my family and all my friends were on board." (Albers, 75) This pleasant cruise was interrupted when the boat became grounded on a sand bar for four days, but the rest of the trip went well. They played cards with other passengers, watched a solar eclipse, stopped in some towns, and observed the scenery. Mitchell noted the arrival of spring and the course of the river: "Today the river banks began to show signs of verdure. On the west bank we saw a tree in bud and wheat looking very pretty. The banks are very changing and at times we seem to be too much surrounded by land to creep out and we go through some narrow defiles where it seems to me that we had better not meet a boat." (Albers, 77)

In New Orleans Mitchell and the Swifts, like typical tourists, visited churches, monuments, and shops. It was Maria's first encounter with one aspect of the South of which she strongly disapproved: slavery. A visit to a slave market made a strong impression on her:

> There was a girl among them . . . who roused my sympathies very much. I could not speak to her, for the past and the future were too plainly told in her face. I spoke to another, a bright looking girl of 12. "Where were you raised?" "In Kentucky." "And why are you to be sold?" "'The trader came to Kentucky and bought me and brought me here." I [thought] what right had I to be homesick when that poor girl had left all her kindred for life, without her consent. (Albers, 79)

Mitchell and Prudie parted from Mr. Swift at New Orleans and continued to tour the Deep South alone. They traveled through Alabama, Georgia, the Carolinas, Tennessee, Kentucky, and Virginia, appreciating natural wonders like the Mammoth Cave and the architectural beauty of Charleston. Although the people she met had political views markedly different from hers, Mitchell found them to be consistently hospitable and kind. "Every one is courteous too in speech; I know they cannot love Massachusetts, but they are so careful not to wound my feelings. They acknowledge it to be the great state in education." (Albers, 81) In Charleston, she noted "Nothing can exceed the hospitality shown to us. We have several invitations for each day and calls without much limit." (Albers, 82) But, in her eyes, Southern culture lacked intellectual rigor—she was disappointed not to be able to find Elizabeth Barrett Browning's poems in any bookstore.

A slave market in Atlanta, photographed during the Civil War. One particularly eye-opening experience for Mitchell was her first visit to a New Orleans slave market like this one. Although she found many of the white people she met in the South to be kind and considerate toward her, the business of separating black families and selling their members to various owners horrified her. Many of her friends, then and later, were abolitionists; after the Civil War ended slavery, their cause tended to shift toward women's rights.

THE CONTINENT

Mitchell and Prudie set off for Europe in late July. Maria was anxious to visit as many observatories and meet as many astronomers in Europe as possible, not merely to see the typical sights. So she obtained letters of introduction to European astronomers from her friends in the United States, among them Edward Everett, Joseph Henry, George P. Bond, and A.D. Bache. The Bonds also gave Mitchell a special prize to take to Europe: one of the earliest photographs of a star. The Harvard men were pioneering the use of photography in astronomy and wished to share this work with astronomers overseas.

When she arrived in Europe, Mitchell discovered that she already had an established reputation and was very well received. In England, Mitchell met many prominent astronomers, mathematicians, and men and women of science. She visited observatories in Liverpool, Greenwich, Cambridge University, and Scotland. She conversed with men whose books had influenced her own work. She made a valuable connection with Sir George B. Airy, the Astronomer Royal. She was invited often to the Airy home in Greenwich and developed a lasting friendship with Mrs. Airy, who showed her the ins and outs of English society. With the Airys, Mitchell not only enjoyed intellectual conversation but also the comfort of a family circle. The Airys introduced her to many other scholars and scientists, among them Frederick G.W. von Struve, the respected head of the Pulkova Observatory in Russia, who had begun the study of binary stars. Before leaving England, Mitchell gave the precious photograph of a star to Airy.

At Cambridge, she met not only astronomers but many members of the faculty, including Dr. William Whewell, the master of Trinity College—one of the few people whom Mitchell actively disliked. Not only did Whewell disparage the work of Ralph Waldo Emerson (whom she knew and respected) and of Elizabeth Barrett Browning (whose poetry she loved), but Mitchell felt that he was rude and spoke sarcastically to others, which offended her. Sir John Herschel and his family, on the other hand, made her very welcome. Sir John had catalogued the stars of the Southern Hemisphere and came from an astronomical family: his father, William, had discovered Uranus and his aunt Caroline had worked closely with the elder Herschel, as Maria did with her father. With the Herschels, Mitchell enjoyed scientific conversation, reminiscences about the elder scientists, and family fun in the evenings. When she left, Sir John gave her a page from Caroline's work with her autograph. "I value [it] extremely," Mitchell wrote. (Mitchell, "Reminiscences," 907)

Between scientific visits, Mitchell took Prudie around London, Stratford-upon-Avon, the Lake Country, and Scotland. They saw dishes being painted at a porcelain factory in Worcester and an entire ox roasted on market day in Warwick. They also watched a debate at the House of Commons, marveled at the great size of St. Paul's Cathedral, and visited the British Museum and the Crystal Palace. At night, they went to dances, parties, and the theater. Although they went to the opera to hear a famous singer of the day, Mitchell did not enjoy it: "The opera fatigued me, as music always does. I tired my eyes

THE ROYAL OBSERVATORY

The Royal Observatory at Greenwich was founded by King Charles II of England in 1675. Sir George B. Airy, Maria Mitchell's friend, was the seventh Astronomer Royal. The observatory was originally established to provide astronomical knowledge that helped sailors navigate, such as information about the position of celestial bodies and ways to determine time. The *Nautical Almanac*, which was first published in 1767, used the longitude of the town of Greenwich for its calculations. This British work came to be used internationally. In 1884, an international agreement officially named the longitude passing through the observatory at Greenwich as the prime meridian or 0° longitude, from which all other longitudes as well as the world's time zones are calculated.

The prestigious Greenwich Observatory, commissioned by King Charles II in June of 1675, was one of the observatories Mitchell visited on her travels; even while working at the Atheneum and teaching herself astronomy, she felt equal in methodology to the Observatory's director. It is famous now as the world standard for time zones and longitude.

and ears in the vain effort to appreciate it." (Albers, 94) She had never had an ear for music, and after her experience in London she decided to stop trying to appreciate it.

While in England, she wanted to visit some places special to her. She wrote, "There are four great men whose haunts I mean to seek out, and on whose footprints I mean to stand: Newton, Shakespeare, Milton, and Johnson." (Albers, 92) She took Prudie to Newton's house with its "little oblong-shaped observatory, built apparently of wood and much blackened by age" (Albers, 93) and to the Royal Society to see his telescope and other instruments. They also walked through narrow London streets and alleys in search of the house in which Dr. Johnson had written his dictionary of the English language and the house in which he had died. In Stratford, they visited Shakespeare's birthplace.

After more than three months of travel together in England, Prudie was forced to go home in early November when the panic of 1857 left her father bankrupt. Mitchell moved on to Paris. "Paris is splendid. The streets like the Champs Élysées and Rue Rivoli are beautiful now, and in summer must be charming." (Albers, 110) While there, she was received by Urbain Leverrier, the head of the Paris Observatory and also a recipient of the Danish medal. Mitchell felt that his poor English and her poor French made it difficult for them to communicate, and they did not develop the comfortable, easy relationship she had enjoyed with the English astronomers. Nonetheless, she was asked to tea at the observatory and was given a tour and introduced to his assistants and family.

In early January, Mitchell was ready to leave Paris. She felt that she needed an escort to go on to Italy and asked to join the author Nathaniel Hawthorne and his family on their journey to Rome. Hawthorne had just finished serving as U.S. consul to Liverpool, and Mitchell had met him when she had first arrived in England. At this point, the Hawthornes were about to start a long vacation to Italy. When she had met Hawthorne in Liverpool, Mitchell had found him eccentric:

> He remained about five minutes, during which time he took his hat from the table and put it back once a minute, brushing it each time. . . . He is not handsome, but he looks as the author of his works should look; a little strange and odd, as if not quite of the earth. . . . [H]is hair stands out on each side, so much, that one's thoughts naturally turn to combs and hair brushes . . . as one looks at him. (Albers, 89)

When she asked to join his family's traveling party, Hawthorne was surprised. He noted in his diary, "We readily consented [to take her], for she seems to be a simple, strong, healthy, humored woman, who will not fling herself as a

The Hawthorne family. Nathaniel Hawthorne, famous author of *The Scarlet Letter*, *The House of Seven Gables*, and other works, became one of Mitchell's friends when they met in Europe and the astronomer accompanied him and his family to Rome. She also developed a close relationship with Hawthorne's children, who called her "Aunt Maria."

burden on our shoulders; and my only wonder is, that a person evidently so able to take care of herself should care about having an escort." (Albers, 114) But Mitchell got along very well with the Hawthornes. Typically, she struck up a friendship with the children, to whom she soon became "Aunt Maria." She introduced Rosa to French gingerbread, gave Julian her lunch on one day's journey through France, and took Una on a carriage ride to Rome's Coliseum. In *The Marble Faun* (1860), a novel inspired by that trip, Hawthorne used Mitchell in his examples of womanhood: "A needle is familiar to the fingers of them all. . . . [T]he woman's eye that has discovered a new star turns from its glory to send the polished little instrument gleaming along the hem of her kerchief, or to darn a casual fray in her dress." (Hawthorne, 36)

Once in Rome, Maria Mitchell found her own lodgings and lived her own life, although she socialized with the Hawthornes and sometimes went sightseeing with them. Mitchell had looked forward to seeing Rome, and it was everything she hoped for from the beginning. She wrote to her sister Phebe, "I am in Rome! I have been here four days, and already I feel that I would rather have that four days in Rome than all the other days of my travels!" (Albers, 116) At the Roman Forum, she felt "as if I dreamed and as if these proofs of the existence of highly cultivated people so many centuries ago could not be actually existing except in my recollections of what I had read. . . . I felt the solemnity of Rome and it seemed to me that a conception of time and of the world's age . . . filled my mind for the first time in my life." (Albers, 117)

Although she mixed with the community of American writers and artists in Rome, she tried to experience Italian culture. In February of 1858, she participated in the daily *Carnevale* festivities, and in March she went to the Holy Week celebrations at the Vatican in spite of the crush of people. Just as her father had taught her, she wanted to see things for herself. She was rather contemptuous of American tourists who "study not the scene before them, but the guide books in their hands. How much better to have read the books in the stormy days at home or to have left them unread." (Wright, 117) Mitchell visited many art galleries as before, but she returned to the Vatican Museum many times. She decided, "No one can look at the statues and paintings of the Vatican without feeling their superiority to all that they have seen before." (Albers, 117)

The Vatican also was the site of the Observatory of the Collegio Romano, which she dearly wanted to visit. This was a difficult to arrange, though, because the observatory was on the grounds of a Jesuit monastery, where women were not allowed to enter. Even Mary Somerville, the most prominent woman scientist of her day, had been refused. Mitchell had been kindly received by astronomers in Rome, including Father Secchi, the observatory director. But admission to the observatory could not take place without permission from the Pope himself. Fortunately, Mitchell met a man with important family connections in the Catholic Church, and her new acquaintance was able to win her the desired invitation. The visit had to take place entirely during the day, but she was able to see the moon and several planets through the telescope and to discuss methods of observation with Father Secchi. Conscious of history, Mitchell mused about the way the Church's views about astronomy had changed since the time of Galileo, who had been condemned by the Church in the 1600s for asserting that the earth revolved around the sun, and not vice versa:

> The circumstance that most interested me was this. Father Secchi's telescope has clockwork made to keep the motion of the earth on its axis—the very motion for asserting whose existence Galileo suffered. The clockwork carries the telescope west to follow the stars just as fast as the earth rolls toward the east. The earth keeps on turning even if the Holy Church did declare that a motion on its axis was absurd in philosophy and erroneous in faith.
>
> And yet it is but a little way . . . from the Hall of Minerva where Galileo was tried to the Collegio Romano where Secchi observes. (Wright, 119)

After two and one half months in Rome, Mitchell began her return trip. She traveled across northern Italy, stopping to visit Mary Somerville, a mathematician and physicist whom Mitchell admired greatly. It was a special treat to discuss the latest editions of her work on physics and the new theories about heat and motion on which she was working. Years later, Mitchell kept a bust of Mrs. Somerville in her observatory. From Italy, she moved through Austria and Germany. In Berlin, she met the great explorer and naturalist Alexander von Humboldt. Although he was at the end of his life, Mitchell

While in Italy, Mitchell visited the Vatican Museum numerous times and was immensely impressed by its collection of art. Mitchell wanted to experience things firsthand, to see for herself, not to be told how things were by a guidebook or someone else—an attitude she inherited from her father that reflects her outlook on science.

found him very well-informed about current events and enthusiastic about science. "No young aspirant in science ever left Humboldt's presence uncheered." (Albers, 127) Finally she reached England again, where she visited the Airys one more time before returning home.

When Maria reached home, she took up the care of her sick mother. Nursing her mother took up most of Mitchell's time,

and the only paying job she had during that time was computing for the *Nautical Almanac*—although she resumed her
astronomical work. While Mitchell was in Europe, friends and
admirers had raised money to buy her a new telescope. The
campaign was successful and, after her return home, she was
able to order a better instrument than she had used before.
After Mrs. Mitchell's death in 1861, William Mitchell resigned
his position at the Pacific Bank and moved with Maria to Lynn,
Massachusetts, to be near Kate and her family. They built a
small observatory in their new home and joined the scientific
activities in the area.

6

Mitchell as Professor: 1862–1869

There is this great danger in student life. Now, we rest all upon what Socrates said, or what Copernicus taught; how can we dispute authority which has come down to us, all established, for ages? We must at least question it; we cannot accept anything as granted, beyond the first mathematical formulae. Question everything else.
—Maria Mitchell, 1874

VASSAR FEMALE COLLEGE

When Matthew Vassar founded Vassar Female College, there were no other colleges that accepted women as students. There were seminaries and normal schools that prepared girls to be grammar school teachers, but no school offered the full courses of study that a college provides. The issue of giving girls a higher education was extremely controversial in the mid-1800s. Some critics said that rigorous study would make young

Vassar Female College was founded in 1861 by Matthew Vassar. Although many members of the faculty were men, Vassar deliberately sought Mitchell to teach astronomy at his new institution, and she became one of only two female instructors there. Although she was paid less than male professors, Mitchell became a stalwart advocate and fundraiser for the college and was much beloved by her students. She retired from Vassar in 1888, but not before lobbying successfully for a raise in her salary.

women lose their femininity and want to be like men. Others said it would damage women's health.

Even those who favored women's higher education often disagreed about the best way to provide it. When Vassar Female College was still being built in the early 1860s, the trustees and supporters debated over the best way to organize it. Some wanted students to wear uniforms; others felt that such a step treated young women like children. The organizers also argued over how to best supervise students. Many thought a male president would not be suitable to direct the girls' personal lives. So the trustees named a "lady principal" who could tell the students how many baths they should take each week and how they were supposed to behave.

Another concern the trustees had was the faculty. They wanted "to build and endow a college for young women which shall be to them, what Yale and Harvard are to young men." (Horowitz, 29) Most of the trustees believed that to have a first-class faculty it was necessary to have only male professors. But Matthew Vassar felt that a college for women should provide female role models for its students. Vassar said, "Let us prove the certainty of woman's higher possible future by the best examples from the present." (Horowitz, 38)

THE PROCESS OF APPOINTMENT

Maria Mitchell became part of this controversy when the trustees began considering her for the position of astronomy professor. In August of 1862, trustee Rufus Babcock approached Mitchell to determine her suitability for the job. He did not, at the time, tell her that this was his intent; he left her thinking that he merely wanted her opinions on women's education. Babcock was clearly impressed by Maria. He wrote to Matthew Vassar after their meeting: "She is by far the most accomplished astronomer of her sex in the world; I have no doubt. And but few of our manly sort are anywhere near her equal. . . . She has moreover a breadth of culture I was by no means prepared to expect." (Albers, 141)

Still, Mitchell had never attended or taught in a college, so she did not have an academic record for Babcock to evaluate. He needed recommendations from people who knew her and who also knew what would be expected of a college professor. Benjamin Peirce, the Harvard mathematician and astronomer with whom she worked on the *Nautical Almanac*, and Alexis Caswell, president of Brown University, sent strong recommendations. Alphonsus Crosby, head of the

State Normal School in Salem, Massachusetts and a friend of Mitchell's, wrote:

> I should consider the Trustees of the Vassar Female College eminently fortunate, if they could secure the services of Miss Maria Mitchell as Professor of Astronomy.
>
> Her distinguished scientific attainments, her liberal literary culture, the remarkable successes & honors which she has already attained, her signal industry & zeal in the promotion of science, her frankness & ease of personal communication, her acquaintance with the institutions & savants of our own & other lands, & her beautiful simplicity & benevolence of character, unite in commending her as preeminently fitted for this position. (Albers, 142)

With these glowing reports supporting his own positive impression, Babcock urged Mitchell's appointment as astronomy professor. Matthew Vassar was immediately enthusiastic about Mitchell's appointment and wrote her, "You will please to excuse me when I say as the Founder of the College that I feel the deepest anxiety for the successful occupancy of that Professorship, and believe there is no one in our Country can better insure it than yourself." (Albers, 145) A warm friendship developed between him and Mitchell that lasted until his death.

That appointment did not happen immediately, though. The college suffered through several construction delays caused by the Civil War. In early 1865, the Board of Trustees finally made a formal offer, but the cost overruns caused by the construction delays had forced the college to reduce the original salary offer of $1,500 to only $800 plus room and board for herself and her father.

THE WORK BEGINS

That September, Vassar College opened to its first class with a faculty of eight professors and 12 teachers who prepared the girls who were not yet ready to do college-level work. Two of the

Matthew Vassar, the founder of his eponymous college, was a wealthy brewer who believed in higher education for women. At the time, this was an unpopular position in society, and many of his contemporaries felt that too much studying would actually cause women to become ill. Vassar was of the contrary opinion, and partly because of his advocacy of women's education he and Mitchell became good friends. His death in 1868 was almost as severe a personal blow to her as the death of her own father.

professors were women—Mitchell and Dr. Alida Avery, who taught physiology and hygiene and served as resident doctor.

One of the three original college buildings was the observatory, which held the third-largest telescope in the United

States at the time. Unfortunately, problems appeared as soon as Mitchell tried to use the instrument. The lens had not been properly ground and details were not clearly visible. Another problem, with the drive mechanism, made the objects being viewed move rather than stay stationary. In spite of its great size, the telescope had no motor to move it into position, so someone had to stand on a ladder and push it into place. Finally, the dome was so heavy that Mitchell could not open the slit for viewing or rotate the dome alone. It took time and money to fix the problems, and it was not until the fall of 1868 that she was able to have the lens reground. For much of her teaching and astronomical work, Mitchell had to depend on smaller telescopes and other instruments.

MATTHEW VASSAR

Matthew Vassar had very little formal education—perhaps two or three years of schooling. But he was intelligent and hardworking, and he became a very successful brewer. With time, he also became the most prominent citizen in Poughkeepsie, New York and personally involved in most of the town's civic affairs. He provided financial support to various projects, among them his church. Although married, Vassar had no children.

He decided he wanted to leave as a legacy a great contribution to society. When the idea of endowing a women's college was proposed to him—something no one had done before—it immediately appealed to him. Having had little formal education, he also had few prejudices against women's ability to learn or teach at the college level. He wanted his college to have the most complete and grandest facility possible and not only built the observatory as well as the huge main building but also purchased almost 1,000 books and an art collection of more than 400 works.

The observatory also presented domestic problems. Mitchell and her father lived in the building, but it was not designed as a living space. The observatory also proved to be cold in winter—a hardship to Maria's aging father. Worse, although Mr. Mitchell had a private bedroom, Maria did not. She had to sleep on a lounge chair in the parlor—a room that students had to pass through to get to the dome. With students going through the room at different times of the day and night, Mitchell had no privacy. When a bedroom was finally built for her in 1875, the event made the school newspaper and was immortalized in a student poem entitled "Miss Mitchell Sleeps in a Bed."

"THE EFFORT TO GRASP GREAT TRUTHS"

In spite of all her accomplishments, Mitchell had some doubts about her ability to be a professor. With her father's encouragement and faith in her to buoy her spirits, she gave an inspirational first lecture to her first class:

> We shall grow larger if we accustom ourselves to contemplate great objects—we shall broaden with the effort to grasp great truths. . . .
>
> There is something elevating in the study of any of the natural sciences, and especially there must be in the study of other worlds. When we are chafed and fretted by small cares, a look at the stars will show us the littleness of our own interests. I would hold out to you the study of nature for its own sake—to learn the truths it can tend you—to get a faint idea of the grandeur of creation and the wonderful working of celestial mechanism. (Wright, 150)

Mitchell gave a series of lectures to sophomores to acquaint them with astronomy, but the rigorous work in astronomy began in the junior year. With the juniors and seniors, there were fewer lectures and more learning by doing—the way she herself had learned. Mitchell gave them individual instruction on the use of astronomical instruments and taught them to find the planets at any hour of the day or night. She had them take measurements and solve problems, such as calculating latitude and longitude, lunar and solar eclipses, the positions of the planets and their moons, and their rotations and orbits. The basis of her teaching was mathematical. Mitchell frequently stressed that astronomy "is not star-gazing. The laws which govern the motions of the sun, the earth, planets, and other bodies in the universe, cannot be understood and demonstrated without a solid basis of mathematical learning." (Wright, 163)

Mitchell wanted her students to become careful observers. They were expected to "make sometimes very accurate drawings and . . . learn to know the satellites of Saturn . . . by their different physiognomy as they would persons"— that is, to become so familiar with heavenly bodies that they could recognize them individually, not just in relation to one another. (Albers, 294) She taught her students to question everything, not to trust even the most recognized authority: "There is this great danger in student life. Now, we rest all upon what Socrates said, or what Copernicus taught; how can we dispute authority which has come down to us, all established, for ages? We must at least question it; we cannot accept anything as granted, beyond the first mathematical formulae. Question everything else." ("Astronomy at Vassar") Much to her delight, Mitchell's students took her at her word. Of her very first class at Vassar, she wrote, "I allow them great freedom of questions and they puzzle me daily. They show more mathematical ability than I had expected and more originality of thought." (Albers, 160)

Mitchell left the instruments set up so her students could use them outside of class during their free time. And she taught them a method of working:

Plan in advance for what you desire to see—good or bad. If you have clouds you have at least gained by thinking it over.

Record—write down all that you do see—good or bad—weak or strong. You need not publish it!

Be honest—avoid the temptation to see what you are expected to see. Do not try to make the eyes catch the objects, but let the objects catch the eye. (Wright, 158)

Through the school and her outside contacts, Mitchell created opportunities for students to do practical astronomy. Students made observations to determine the college's location, which information was used to set the college clocks; they wrote a regular column about the astronomical events of the month for *Scientific Monthly;* and they kept meteorological records for the Smithsonian Institution. She also involved students in her research, watching and photographing sunspots. They photographed Mercury and Venus moving across the face of the sun. Students joined her to count meteors during a meteor shower and subsequently published their results. In 1869 and 1878, she took groups of students to observe a total eclipse of the sun.

Sometimes Mitchell provided a change of pace in class by telling them about the lives and work of other astronomers and scientists—many of whom she had known. She told them stories about Kepler and Galileo, the Herschels, Humboldt, and Mary Somerville. She also talked of how science had changed over the centuries and how it was portrayed in early myths and in the works of Shakespeare and Milton. Mitchell did not expect all of her students of become astronomers, but she wanted them to see how humanity's understanding of science influenced its understanding of society; how failure led scientists to new discoveries; and how great the universe was. She wanted students to learn to think and to question what they saw and heard.

Maria Mitchell carried out other professorial activities along with her teaching. She continued to study and read new works in mathematics, astronomy and other sciences. She published the results of her research and gave lectures to members of different organizations, college audiences, lyceums, and alumni groups. Lecturing gave her an opportunity to travel to different parts of the country and, by 1871, earned her more money than teaching at Vassar. Nonetheless, Mitchell's principal commitment was to Vassar.

At Vassar, she quickly developed a reputation as a demanding and blunt but very kind teacher. She did not tolerate careless work and let her students know when their work was not up to her standards. On the other hand, she made a point of visiting students who were not used to being away from home to make sure they felt comfortable. Indeed, for many students, the Observatory became a home away from home, and Mitchell and her father became surrogate parents. Maria invited the senior students in particular to bring their friends to see how the instruments worked—as long as the guests did not touch them. The Mitchells took a personal interest in the young women, many of whom confided in them. Some students even visited them over vacation.

A unique feature of life at Vassar were Maria's "dome parties." At the end of each academic year, the interior of the observatory's dome was decorated and the astronomy students were invited for a special breakfast or lunch. Mitchell would recite a short, humorous poem she had written about each student and a longer piece about the entire group. The group reciprocated with their own verses to Maria, sung to the tune of "The Battle Hymn of the Republic"—a song composed during the Civil War to verses of Mitchell's friend Julia Ward Howe.

LIBERATING THE STUDENT

Just as she taught her students to be honest in their astronomical work, Mitchell was an example of honesty in her life. The girls

Mitchell standing among colleagues, students, and telescopes—her natural surroundings. For years she served as an inspiration to other young astronomers through her kind yet demanding teaching methods and her intense intellect. She made it her mission to spread her learning to those around her and created unprecedented educational opportunities for women, especially in astronomy.

were not the only ones who heard exactly what she thought of their work, college administrators did, too. Mitchell refused to take attendance in class because it went against her ideas of individual freedom. She objected to having to give grades and once mocked the grading system, in which "5" was the highest grade:

> If a girl has faithfully studied her lesson and does not know it, she deserves 5 for her industry. If she has not studied, yet knows it, she deserves 5 for her intellect. If she has neither studied nor knows it, she deserves 5 for her audacity in coming before me so. (Wright, 169)

Mitchell encouraged her students to protest unnecessary rules—such as those governing how they should bite their bread or when they could cross their feet. In her diary, she wrote, "How much have I a right to influence students to petition for changes, in the College discipline. I really and truly believe that the girls here submit too much to rule, that they should combine and protest against some of the petty laws." (Albers, 237) And Mitchell would not hesitate to break rules by getting her students out of bed after "lights out" to observe a comet or other astronomical event.

Mitchell's students appreciated what she taught them and who she was. One inspired student explained that "in Miss Mitchell's classroom computations became sublime and logarithms were transformed from dry bones to living spirits, leading the soul out into limitless space, past seen and unseen systems to the great center of the universe." (Wright, 164) A former student wrote to her, "Not all the lessons I learned have been forgotten. . . . Many of them have been the inspiration of all that I have accomplished of any worth. I have wished many times to tell you or in some way to show you how deeply I feel this." Another former student paid her tribute by naming her first daughter Maria Mitchell.

Early in her years at Vassar, Mitchell suffered two great losses. Matthew Vassar died in 1868. Mitchell believed that his moral authority had been a strong, positive influence on the college. "We could not afford to lose Mr. Vassar," she wrote, "although we gained $300,000." (Wright, 181) Her father's death in the following year was a tremendous personal loss. William Mitchell had been her support and companion for many years. They had shared their work, friends, and family life. Maria now faced "the new and incomprehensible life" before her alone. (Albers, 176)

7

Carrying the Torch for Women: 1869–1876

It seems to me that the [sewing or embroidery] needle is the chain of woman, and has fettered her more than the laws of the country.

Once emancipate her from the 'stitch, stitch, stitch,' . . . and she would have time for studies which would engross as the needle never can.
—Maria Mitchell, diary entry, February 15, 1853

After her father's death, Mitchell plunged into work to promote educational and work opportunities for women. Her views on these subjects had been forming for years. In her Atheneum days, Mitchell had been acutely conscious of difference in the education men and women received. In 1853, she had written:

> The art of sewing . . . is well enough; that is, to enable a person to take the stitches, and, if necessary, to make her own garments in a strong manner; but the dressmaker should

By the 1860s, Mitchell was gaining fame not only as an astronomer but also as a feminist. At Vassar, she was a champion of giving women a thorough education equal to that which men received, and she also worked in the movement for women's suffrage. She was a natural example of a woman's capacity to achieve at least as much as a man.

no more be a universal character than the carpenter.

Suppose every man should feel it is his duty to do his own mechanical work of all kinds, would society be benefited? Would the work be well done? Yet a woman is expected to know how to do all kinds of sewing, all kinds of cooking, all kinds of any woman's wok, and the consequence is that life is passed in learning these only, while the universe of truth beyond remains unentered. (Albers, 41)

By 1868, Mitchell felt completely committed to Vassar and to work for the betterment of women. In her diary, she wrote, "(Resolved) In case of my outliving Father and being in good health, to give my efforts to the intellectual culture of women, without regard to salary." (Albers, 171) Indeed, she found herself having to defend the existence of Vassar College itself after the publication of Edward Clarke's *Sex in Education* in 1873. In that book, Clarke claimed that the health of several Vassar students had been damaged by their studies. Mitchell wrote letters of protest to magazines.

Once resolved, Mitchell entered into her work for women's rights with the full force of her intellect and personality. Frances A. Wood, a friend and colleague at Vassar, explained, "However interested you might have been in woman suffrage and all the other subjects concerning the 'cause,' you felt that in comparison with this grand woman you hardly knew the alphabet. She judged everything from the standpoint, 'How is this going to affect women?'" (Albers, 221) Because of her stature as a scientist, women's rights advocates had for years used Mitchell as an example of what women could achieve. When she became active in the cause, Mitchell soon became an acknowledged feminist leader.

In lectures and articles, Mitchell called for equal opportunities for women. "To discuss the question whether women have the capacity for original investigation in science is simply idle until equal opportunity is given them," she wrote. (Mitchell, 908) To emphasize her point, Mitchell used the example of Caroline Herschel, whose great gifts went to waste after her brother's death because she was unable to carry on research by herself.

On the other hand, Mitchell was equally critical of women who did nothing to improve themselves or their situation. In a lecture at Vassar, she told her students:

Are we women using all the rights we have? We have the right to steady and continuous effort after knowledge, after truth. Who denies our right to life-long study? Yet you will find most women leave their studies when they leave the schoolroom. . . .

We have another right, which I am afraid we do not use, the right to do our work well, *as well as men do theirs.* . . . I am almost ready to say that women do their work less thoroughly than men. Perhaps from the need of right training, perhaps because they enter upon occupations only temporarily, they keep school a year, they write one magazine article. . . .

And this seems to me woman's greatest wrong, the wrong which she does to herself by work loosely done, ill finished, or not finished at all. The world has not yet outgrown the idea that women are playthings, because women have not outgrown it themselves. (Albers, 198–199)

In 1873, Mitchell took a second trip to Europe in which she not only visited scientists but also women's schools in England, Germany, Russia, and Switzerland. She found women's education in a worse state there than in the United States. Her views of women's unwillingness to improve themselves were confirmed by a group of Russian women she met who described themselves as being in favor of women's rights and asked her many questions about Vassar. Mitchell "begged them to study by themselves and so hold up a lesson for women. They said, 'The Russians have not the energy of the Americans.'" (Albers, 216) In Cambridge, England she spoke with a woman who ran a house for girls who studied with the professors at the university. To Mitchell's dismay, the woman completely left "*to the Professors* the decision of what studies are *suitable for women.*" (Albers, 207) Mitchell was encouraged by her visit to Girton College for women at Cambridge University, where one of the founders "has obtained a quiet power that is very effective." (Albers, 208)

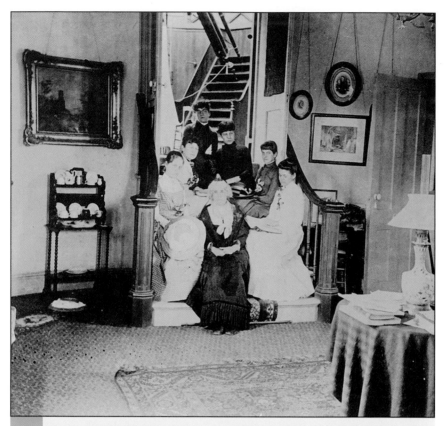

Mitchell was an inspiration to her students at Vassar, and she traveled around the country and in Europe to promote higher education for women. She also encouraged her students to study on their own as well as in the classroom in order to achieve their full intellectual potential.

In the United States, Mitchell promoted increasing educational opportunities for women. Since the 1860s, she had urged the acceptance of women at men's schools like Harvard and Cornell, and she stayed informed about the women's colleges that were springing up. In 1879, she asked a friend about progress at Smith College, another new women's school, and learned that it had "a great many special students." Mitchell recalled, "I asked her if they had students who knew no Latin and she said, 'Oh, yes.' I asked her if there were careful examinations before they were passed from class to class and she said, 'Oh no. We are hardly systematized yet enough for that.'" (Albers, 225) Given Mitchell's strong views, she was undoubtedly unhappy with these responses. When she visited the Harvard Annex for women in 1880—the school that later became Radcliffe College—she found their education to be inferior to the young men's. She judged the mathematics class to be below the college level and to be poorly taught. Moreover, "The Lecturer in Physics has no apparatus, nor has he of Chemistry so that the Boys at Harvard have very much greater advantages than the Girls of the Annex." (Albers, 266) In the end, Mitchell came to believe that "a better way is co-education." (Albers, 316)

Ironically, although she taught at a women's college, Mitchell found herself having to fight discrimination against women faculty. Even at Vassar, women faculty were not initially assigned to academic committees, they were completely over-looked when the president requested a list of faculty publica-tions, and they were paid far less than male faculty members. In 1867, male professors were paid $2,500, but Mitchell only received $800 plus room and board for herself and her father. The salary dispute took years to resolve. Dr. Alida Avery voiced her objections together with Mitchell. At one stage, the two informed the president that they would resign if the situation were not resolved. In a joint letter to President Raymond dated May of 1870, they wrote:

> We desire to call your attention to the fact, that, after nearly five years of what we believe to be faithful working for the good of the College, our pay is still far below that which has been offered at entrance, to the other professors, even when they have been wholly inexperienced. (Albers, 200)

Mitchell was the most renowned professor at Vassar, and during the time of the dispute, the college rebuffed Swarthmore College's request that she teach there. Eventually, the two professors had to appeal to a sympathetic trustee to pressure

During her lifetime, Mitchell met and befriended many prominent writers and scholars, including the poet Julia Ward Howe, who was an abolitionist and also her co-vice president in the Association for the Advancement of Women and who often wrote about her famous astronomer friend. Howe is probably known best for her poem "The Battle Hymn of the Republic" (1862), which became the text of one of the most powerful songs of the Civil War.

the Executive Committee of the college to treat them more reasonably. Mitchell later explained in a letter to that trustee that neither one of them wanted more money out of personal concerns: "At the time . . . Dr. Avery and I were fighting for all women, for it was more the general than the special injustice that reached us." (Albers, 201)

FINANCIAL DIFFICULTIES AT VASSAR

By the 1870s, Vassar, like other colleges, found itself without enough money to continue funding its programs fully. Mitchell pitched in to do fundraising for the school. At her public lectures, she asked members of the audience to give endowments or gifts to colleges. In the 1880s her appeals focused on preserving the observatory and the professorship of astronomy at Vassar. Mitchell asked for money from Vassar alumnae, from her personal friends, and from anyone else she thought might have something to give. Her results were mixed. Contributions ranged from $25 to thousands, although some people did not give at all. Over time, Mitchell even began to enjoy asking for money:

> I have given myself over to Mammon—i.e. am begging for the Obs[servatory] of Vassar and am pulling wires. I have taken about $2700 add a zero and I will have done with such work forever.
>
> But I've had a good time, seen lots of nice people whom it would have been a pity not to know. (Albers, 295)

Mitchell became increasingly forceful in putting forth her ideas. As more women's colleges were founded, questions about naming women to the faculties and boards of trustees continued to arise. Mitchell wrote to the board of the new Bryn Mawr College in 1880 to inquire about the lack of women trustees, the probability that women would be appointed to the faculty, and the study of astronomy at the college—all of her important causes.

Similar issues continued to trouble Vassar. In 1881, the founder's nephew, Matthew Vassar Jr., died and left $80,000 to the college to endow professorships—but stipulated that only men could be named to those chairs. A controversy ensued over the morality of a women's college accepting such a bequest. Mitchell argued that the school should stick to its principles and refuse the money, but others felt that, since the school needed the money and good male professors would benefit women, it was foolish to refuse it. In the end, the trustees accepted the bequest.

Maria Mitchell worked for women's rights outside of education as well. She gave lyceum talks to women's groups and

ELIZABETH CADY STANTON AND WOMEN'S RIGHTS

Elizabeth Cady Stanton studied law under her father, a U.S. congressman and member of the New York State Supreme Court. After seeing women delegates rejected at the World Anti-Slavery Convention in 1840, she worked tirelessly for women's rights. By means of speeches and petitions, she was instrumental in causing a law to be passed in New York state in 1848 that gave married women property rights.

That same year, she and Lucretia Mott organized the Seneca Falls Convention, which featured Stanton's Declaration of Sentiments, protesting the inferior status of women. She called for numerous reforms and for woman suffrage.

For the next 50 years, Stanton worked together with Susan B. Anthony, planning conventions, giving speeches, and writing articles and pamphlets. An 1854 speech Stanton gave before the New York State legislature inspired laws that made women joint guardians of their children with their husbands and gave them the right to control their own earnings. In 1869, Stanton and Anthony founded the National Woman Suffrage Association, a controversial but influential organization that pushed for voting rights for women. Stanton was its president until 1890, when it merged with the American Woman Suffrage Association. She served as head of the new organization until 1892.

In 1878, Stanton wrote the woman suffrage amendment to the U.S. Constitution that was introduced at every Congress. In 1920, it was finally ratified and women obtained the vote.

Elizabeth Cady Stanton was a prominent figure in the women's rights movement of the mid–19th century. Although Mitchell's ideas on suffrage were not as radical as those of Stanton and Susan B. Anthony, she nevertheless felt that gaining the right to vote was an important goal.

attended political action meetings held by different women's organizations. She had many prominent friends. Among them were novelist Louisa May Alcott, who was trying to get women the vote in Massachusetts; the poet Julia Ward Howe; the suffragist Elizabeth Cady Stanton; the minister Mary Livermore, who believed obtaining woman suffrage was the key to achieving other social reforms; and the fiery abolitionist and reformer Anna Dickinson. According to Frances Wood:

> [All] woman speaker[s] of note in that day . . . were personal friends of Miss Mitchell, and at various times her guests at the observatory. Sometimes one would be invited to speak before the whole college, as when Mrs. Howe recited her "Battle Hymn of the Republic" and Mrs. Livermore told the story of her [Civil War] experiences in a hospital. But the observatory was chiefly the place of meeting, with spirited talk and free discussion. (Albers, 221)

Mitchell also numbered some of her own former students as allies in the fight for women's rights.

THE ASSOCIATION FOR THE ADVANCEMENT OF WOMEN

Mitchell made her most significant contributions to women's rights through the Association for the Advancement of Women (AAW). The organization was founded at a Congress of Women held in New York City in the fall of 1873. Its aim was to promote women's achievement through a yearly conference where there "shall be presented the best ideas and the most advantageous methods of our foremost thinkers and writers. Therefore, we solicit the presence and responsive words of all accordant associations of women—of Women Preachers, Teachers, Professors, Physicians, Artists, Lawyers, Trading Capitalists, Editors, Authors, and Practical Philanthropists, those who by their example inspire others not only to covet the best gifts, but to labor earnestly for them." (Wright, 197) Less radical than the National Woman Suffrage Association founded by Susan B. Anthony and Elizabeth Cady Stanton—which urged giving women the right to vote immediately—the AAW took the view that women would get the vote once they showed they were "capable of work that involved the highest intellectual and social responsibility." (Wright, 197) Mary Livermore was elected president of the association for the first year, and Maria Mitchell and Julia Ward Howe vice presidents. The press gave that first women's congress very positive reviews.

During her own term as president of the AAW, Mitchell promoted the gathering of statistical information about women. In her opening speech, she said, "If we knew the number of girls who have died from overstudy, let us find the number who have died from aimless lives." (Wright, 199) She also promoted trying new approaches in their work. "We are all afraid of new experiments, as if the law of growth through failure were not similar in moral, mental, and material work. There is not a worker in physical science who has not ruined lenses and wasted chemicals; . . . but he knows perfectly well that he has grown with the effort; that his true theory, if he has found one, has started up from the graves of a score of enterprises." (Wright, 200)

Mitchell served as an officer and helped to organize the work of the association over the years. She was a speaker on more than one occasion, but gave the speech closest to her heart at the group's fourth national meeting, held in 1876. The speech was entitled "The Need of Women in Science," and in it Mitchell voiced her belief that women had a special fitness for scientific work because their patience and attention to detail were precisely the skills a scientist needed. As long as women were forced to dedicate their lives to day-to-day concerns, she said, it would be impossible for them to realize their potential:

> The laws of nature are not discovered by accidents; theories do not come by chance, even to the greatest minds; they are not born of the hurry and worry of daily toil; they are diligently sought, they are patiently waited for. . . . And until able women have given their lives to investigation, it is idle to discuss the question of their capacity for original work. (Albers, 243)

The press hailed her speech as a great success. One paper described Mitchell as the AAW's "dignified President— philosophical and wise in statement." (Wright, 203)

8

The Force of Personal Character

As with all true teachers, it was the force of her personal character that acted most upon the young women with whom she came in contact. No one of them but was lifted and strengthened by her strength, sincerity, and single-heartedness.
—Anna C. Brackett, 1889

By and large, Maria Mitchell got along well with the faculty and staff of Vassar College. After a rocky start with the first president, J.H. Raymond, the two developed mutual respect and friendship, although she felt he never wholly gave women their due. After Raymond's death, Samuel L. Caldwell was appointed president, and soon after that one of the trustees, Nathan Bishop, attempted to have Mitchell and another professor ousted from the faculty on religious grounds. Even though Matthew Vassar, the founder, and many of the trustees were Baptists, the college had been established as a non-sectarian

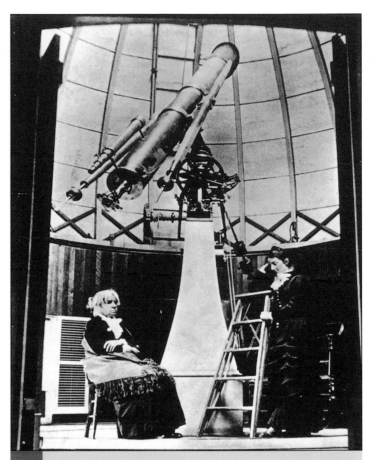

Mitchell sits in the observatory at Vassar while one of her best students, Mary Whitney, peers through the eyepiece. When Mitchell first arrived at Vassar, she found the telescope to be useless because the lens had not been ground correctly, and it was some time before she could actually use it for observations. Whitney became Mitchell's assistant in 1881, and in 1888 she succeeded Mitchell as director of the observatory.

institution. Bishop had been a strong supporter of appointing women as professors, so his objections to Maria Mitchell as well as to Truman Backus clearly were not on sexist grounds. In March of 1879, he wrote to Caldwell,

> I am extremely sorry to learn that Prof. Backus has manifested so bold "Skeptical" [religious] views that a committee of Trustees waited on him before you were elected. I was aware that Miss Mitchell was a "Rank Theodore Parker Unitarian" when she was elected. I believe she has kept away from Vassar five times as many students as her influence has drawn to it. (Albers, 254)

Although the two professors must have gone through serious unpleasantness, neither was removed from the faculty, and Mitchell maintained cordial relations with Caldwell.

MITCHELL'S UNITARIANISM

Like many other Friends who had moved away from strict Quakerism, Mitchell had become a Unitarian. Frances Wood described the small Unitarian community on campus:

> There were only four or five of us outside of the students who had Unitarian preferences, and we were considered on account of this, by our orthodox sisters, to be indeed very black sheep religiously. The club was very informal, . . . entertaining . . . any guests visiting the college that Miss Mitchell considered in sympathy enough to invite. The aim was serious, excluding all gossip and light talk and while there was no straining after "high thinking," it was certain we had frequent hint of this in Miss Mitchell's independent, stimulating opinions, and from . . . guests, bringing their best thoughts with them. . . . She had a deeply religious nature. (Albers, 222)

For Mitchell, her work also had a deeply religious nature: "Every formula which expresses a law of nature is a hymn of praise to God." ("Astronomy of Vassar") Dr. James Monroe Taylor, the last college president with whom Mitchell worked, was a good friend who appreciated the nature of her beliefs. In the eulogy he delivered at her funeral service, he explained, "She would not use the language of faith often because it did not seem to her that she had clearly grasped the truths which came through faith. . . . It would be a grave error to infer from this that she was not a *religious* woman in a true sense. She was always a seeker for *truth*. . . . But she would not allow herself to say one word beyond what she felt she really *knew*." (Albers, 325)

In the 1880s, Mitchell maintained a busy schedule of teaching, research, and work for women's rights. Her fundraising also required a great deal of attention. But her enthusiasm was unflagging. In July of 1881, on a boat to Providence, Rhode Island, on her way home for the summer holiday, Mitchell saw a comet in the sky. She got off the boat and returned to Poughkeepsie as fast as possible to observe the comet. Unfortunately,

UNITARIANISM

American Unitarianism began as a counter-movement to the Great Awakening on the part of Congregationalist ministers. These ministers objected to the emphasis placed on original sin and human depravity by fiery ministers like Jonathan Edwards. Unitarians did not accept any creed or dogma, but rather depended on a person's reasoning and moral conscience to determine his or her individual beliefs. Although this idea might appeal to Quakers who came from a tradition that emphasized the guidance of the Inner Light, to evangelical Christians who believed that the Bible was the ultimate authority, it sounded like no religion at all. Moreover, Unitarians hold that God is one entity, not a Trinity; Jesus, therefore, must be human. And Unitarians also tolerate different forms of worship. Although most Unitarians considered themselves Christians, it was not necessary to be a Christian to be a Unitarian. For many practicing Christians in the 19th century, this was a serious failing.

when she was stationed at her post in the observatory, she was still unable to see the comet. It was low in the sky, and, according to her diary, "a scraggy apple tree" was blocking her view. Mitchell asked the watchman to cut off some branches so she could see. But the first few branches were not enough. When the watchman realized he would have to chop down the entire tree, she told him to cut it down, worrying all the while that there might be a bird's nest in it. She returned to her observation. The next morning at breakfast, Mitchell discovered she had a new reputation on campus—people greeted her by the name "George Washington." (Albers, 275; Wright, 160)

THE DECLINE

In 1881, Mary Whitney became Mitchell's assistant at the observatory. Whitney had been a member of Mitchell's original astronomy class at Vassar and afterward studied with Benjamin Peirce at Harvard. She had also done further work at the University of Zurich in mathematics and celestial mechanics. Whitney was an accomplished astronomer in her own right and an invaluable collaborator to Mitchell as both a teacher and a researcher. When she retired from Vassar in 1888, Mitchell recommended to President Taylor that Whitney be named her successor, and to Frances Wood she described Whitney as "the most powerful rival that I could put in my place and I can only say 'Good luck to her! May she surpass her Teacher and that by many times.'" (Albers, 319)

But even with Whitney to shoulder some of the workload, Mitchell found she needed her summers away from Vassar and her other work. She took vacations on Nantucket, where she could relax and visit with family. She wrote to a friend, "I live mostly on the piazza here. . . . The ocean touches our backyard fence and I sleep by the sound of the surf." (Wright, 217) She also spent time in Lynn, where she enjoyed her sister Kate's children.

In the fall of 1880, Mitchell suffered a bout of pharyngitis and malaria that lasted about six months. She was under her sister Anne's care for some of that time, and Mary Whitney substituted for her. After her recovery, Mitchell remained healthy for the next eight years, suffering only the problems of growing age.

During the Christmas break of 1887–1888, however, she found herself so debilitated that she was forced to resign her position. President Taylor responded that her resignation "has come unexpectedly, undesired—and I would add unwelcomed." (Albers, 304) The Vassar Board of Trustees acted with great consideration toward Mitchell. They refused to act on her resignation until June, and gave her a leave of absence instead, thus allowing her to continue receiving her full salary for several months more. When the Board finally accepted her resignation, it named her Professor Emerita of Astronomy with the right to a residence in the college and the use of the observatory for life.

Meanwhile, Mitchell stayed with her sister and brother-in-law in Lynn. An observatory was built for her in their backyard. She continued to receive offers to lecture, but she declined them. She lived an unusually passive life, and did not even use the observatory for serious study. She continued to keep a diary and to correspond with old friends for some months. Mitchell's health continued to decline, however, and she died one month before her 71st birthday, on June 28, 1889. President Taylor officiated at her funeral.

MITCHELL'S LEGACY

Maria Mitchell left a significant legacy to Vassar, to science, and to women. Her fundraising work ultimately led to the establishment of the Alumnae Maria Mitchell Chair of Astronomy in 1886. The endowment guarantees that Vassar will always have an astronomy professor on its faculty. Appropriately, Mary Whitney was the first person to hold this chair. Mitchell also bequeathed to Vassar her method of teaching astronomy. Although the college has a new observatory, completed in 1997, today's students continue to learn by doing.

Mitchell spent much of her later years fundraising for Vassar and championing women's rights. Highly respected for her contributions to science, even in the male-dominated society of the time, she was the first woman elected to be a member of the American Academy of Arts and Sciences and the American Association for the Advancement of Science.

Mitchell also influenced the lives of many of her students, not only future astronomers like Mary Whitney, but also the physicist and philosopher Christine Ladd-Franklin and the chemist Ellen Swallow Richards, founder of the field of home economics. Some of Mitchell's former students also became active in women's rights. But her influence extended beyond her immediate students. Anna C. Brackett reminisced,

> The special students in astronomy were never very many, but her influence was not confined to them. She took her meals in the large hall and was familiar with all the

students, and wherever she appeared there blew a fresh breeze of genuine life. . . . Her absolute truthfulness of character never failed to find and fortify the honest intent, never missed striking and banishing all affectation. (954)

And her influence was passed on through generations. The son of a former student explained his mother's philosophy: "Never just look at an object. Wonder about it! Wonder who made it, and how. Above all, wonder how it might be improved. Never cease to wonder." (Wright, 236) Clearly, Mitchell's message was being passed on.

As a scholar, Mitchell studied not only comets, eclipses, and binary stars but also nebulae and the moons of Jupiter and Saturn. She did some of the earliest work using photography to study sunspots, by which she identified their structure. She published articles in scientific journals and edited other scientists' works. Inspired by her achievements, the Maria Mitchell Association of Nantucket today helps young people learn astronomy. It provides internships to college students to use its observatory for research and helps them publish and present their results to the scientific community. The Association also grants the annual Maria Mitchell Women in Science Award to encourage women to achieve in science.

Although several generations of women scientists after Mitchell continued to struggle for recognition and jobs, her life proved that women could do high-level work. For many decades, most women astronomers were restricted to computing work at observatories like the United States Naval Observatory and the Harvard Observatory. Generally, they were paid less than men and had fewer opportunities for advancement. The second women's rights movement of the 1960s and after, though, spurred women's interest and participation in science. Today, women work for observatories, scientific journals, and the space program. For all of them, Maria Mitchell blazed the trail.

Chronology

1818   Born on August 1 to William Mitchell and Lydia Coleman Mitchell on Nantucket Island.

1831   Assists her father as he observes a solar eclipse.

1835   Opens her school on Nantucket.

1836   Becomes librarian of the Nantucket Atheneum.

1846   Fire sweeps through Nantucket, destroying the Atheneum.

1847   On October 1, becomes the first person to see the comet now named for her.

1848   Receives gold medal from King of Denmark for sighting her comet; elected as first female member of American Academy of Arts and Sciences.

1849   Hired as a computer for *The American Ephemeris and Nautical Almanac.*

1850   Elected to the American Association for the Advancement of Science.

1857–1858   Travels throughout the southern United States and Europe.

1859   With the help of fundraising by friends and supporters, Mitchell buys a new telescope.

1861   Lydia Mitchell dies; Mitchell and her father move to Lynn, Massachusetts.

1865   Is appointed as Vassar Female College's first professor of astronomy; moves with her father to Poughkeepsie to reside in the college observatory.

1868	Matthew Vassar dies; Mitchell resigns her position with the *Nautical Almanac* to concentrate on teaching at Vassar.
1869	William Mitchell dies.
1875	Elected president of Association for Advancement of Women.
1878	Travels to Denver with her sister and a group of Vassar students travel to view a solar eclipse.
1888	Resigns her professorship.
1889	Dies on June 28 in Lynn, Massachusetts.

Bibliography

Albers, Henry, ed. *Maria Mitchell: A Life in Journals and Letters.* Clinton Corners, N.Y.: College Avenue Press, 2001.

"Astronomy at Vassar," Vassar College, Physics and Astronomy Department website. *physicsandastronomy.vassar.edu/astronomy.shtml.*

Brackett, Anna C. "Maria Mitchell," *The Century* (October 1889): 954.

"The Coming Total Eclipse," *The New York Times,* July 28, 1878.

"Dark Doings," *The New York Times,* July 28, 1878.

"Denver Eclipse," *The Daily Rocky Mountain News* (Denver), July 30, 1878.

Hamm, Thomas D. *The Transformation of American Quakerism: Orthodox Friends, 1800–1907.* Bloomington: Indiana University Press, 1988.

Hawthorne, Nathaniel. *The Marble Faun.* New York: New American Library, 1961.

Horowitz, Helen Lefkowitz. *Alma Mater: Design and Experience in the Women's Colleges from Their Nineteenth-Century Beginnings to the 1930s.* New York: Knopf, 1984.

Maria Mitchell Association website. *www.mmo.org.*

Merriam, Eve, ed. *Growing Up Female in America: Ten Lives.* New York: Dell Publishing Company, 1971.

Mitchell, Maria. "Reminiscences of the Herschels," *The Century* (October 1889): 903–909.

———, Report on the Denver eclipse, 1878. In Henry Albers, ed. *Maria Mitchell: A Life in Journals and Letters.* Clinton Corners, N.Y.: College Avenue Press, 2001, ch. 11.

"Nantucket: Insider's Guide to Cape Cod" website. *www.insiders.com/capecod/main-nantucket2.htm.*

Office of Coast Survey websit. *www.nos.noaa.gov/programs/ocs.html.*

Reingold, Nathan, ed. *The Sciences in the American Context: New Perspectives.* Washington, D.C.: Smithsonian Institution Press, 1979.

Struik, Dirk J. *Yankee Science in the Making.* Boston: Little, Brown, 1948.

Virtual American Biographies website (containing biographies from the 1886 edition of *Appleton's Encyclopedia*). *www.famousamericans.net.*

Wright, Helen. *Sweeper in the Sky: The Life of Maria Mitchell.* Clinton Corners, N.Y.: College Avenue Press, 1997.

Further Reading

Camp, Carole Ann. *American Astronomers: Searchers and Wonderers.* Springfield, N.J.: Enslow Publishers, 1996.

Cobb, Allan B. *How Do We Know How Stars Shine?* New York: Rosen Publishing Group, 2001.

Cooney, Miriam P., ed. *Celebrating Women in Mathematics and Science.* Reston, Va.: National Council of Teachers of Mathematics, 1996.

Davis, Kenneth C. *Don't Know Much About Space.* New York: HarperCollins Publishers, 2001.

Ekrutt, Joachim W. *Stars and Planets: Identifying Them, Learning About Them, Experiencing Them.* Hauppauge, N.Y.: Barron's, 2000.

Gormley, Beatrice. *Maria Mitchell: The Soul of an Astronomer.* Grand Rapids, Mich.: Eerdmans Publishing Company, 1995.

Hoople, Cheryl G. *As I Saw It: Women Who Lied the American Adventure.* New York: Dial Press, 1978.

Levy, David H. *Cosmic Discoveries: The Wonders of Astronomy.* Amherst, N.Y.: Prometheus Books, 2001.

Night Sky: An Explore Your World Handbook. New York: Discovery Books, 1999.

Pasachoff, Jay M. *A Field Guide to the Stars and Planets.* Boston: Houghton Mifflin, 2000.

Stille, Darlene R. *Extraordinary Women Scientists.* Chicago: Childrens Press, 1995.

Stott, Carole. *1,001 Facts About Space.* New York: DK Publishing, 2002.

Vance, Marguerite. *The Lamp Lighters: Women in the Hall of Fame.* New York: Dutton, 1960.

Warren, Rebecca Lowe, and Mary H. Thompson. *The Scientist Within You: Experiments and Biographies of Distinguished Women in Science.* Eugene, Ore.: ACI Publishers, 1994.

Wills, Susan. *Astronomy: Looking at Stars.* Minneapolis: Oliver Press, 2000.

Wilsdon, Christina. *The Solar System: An A–Z Guide.* New York: Franklin Watts, 2000.

Yount, Lisa. *Contemporary Women Scientists.* New York: Facts On File, 1994.

Further Reading

Websites

The Maria Mitchell Association of Nantucket
www.mmo.org

The Woman Astronomer
www.womanastronomer.com/women_astronomers.htm

StarGazing with Jack Horkheimer
www.odysseymagazine.com/pages/Stargazer.html

American Physical Society: Internet Resources for Women Scientists
www.neci.nec.com/homepages/thio/cswp.html

Astronomy.com
www.astronomy.com

Astronomy for Kids
www.dustbunny.com/afk/

Astronomy Now Online
www.astronomynow.com

Kids Astronomy.com
www.kidsastronomy.com

The National Aeronautics and Space Administration
www.nasa.gov

Odyssey: Adventures in Science
www.odysseymagazine.com

The Smithsonian Astrophysical Observatory
www.harvard.edu/sao-home.html

The Hubble Project
hubble.nasa.gov

Vassar College, Physics and Astronomy Department
physicsandastronomy.vassar.edu/astronomy.shtml

The Association for Women in Science
1200 New York Ave., Suite 650NW
Washington, D.C. 20005
www.awis.org

Index

Abolitionist movement, 41
Agassiz, Louis, 35
Airy, Mr. and Mrs. George B., 33, 59
Alcott, Louisa May, 89
Alumnae Maria Mitchell Chair of
    Astronomy, 97
American Academy of Arts and
    Sciences, 49-50
American Association for the
    Advancement of Science, 50
*American Ephemeris and Nautical
    Almanac,* 50, 54
American Journal of Science, The, 27
*American Journal of Science and Arts,
    The,* 51
American Philosophical Society, 50
Anthony, Susan B., 90
Association for the Advancement of
    Women (AAW), 90-91
Audubon, John James, 35
Austria, Mitchell in, 65
Avery, Dr. Alida, 72, 85, 86

Babcock, Rufus, 70, 71
Bache, Alexander Dallas, 46, 50-51,
    52, 59
Backus, Truman, 93
Binary stars, 51
Bishop, Nathan, 92, 93-94
Bond, George P., 32, 46, 47, 48, 49, 59
Bond, William C., 31, 46, 48, 49, 59
Bowditch, Nathaniel, 33
Brackett, Anna C., 98-99
Brontë, Emily, 35
Browning, Elizabeth Barrett, 57, 59
Bryn Mawr College, 87

Caldwell, Samuel L., 92, 93-94
Cambridge University
    Mitchell and, 59-60, 83
    observatory of, 59
Caswell, Alexis, 70
Channing, William Ellery, 35

Chicago, Mitchell in, 55-56
Chronometers
    and 1831 solar eclipse, 27
    and 1878 solar eclipse, 13, 16, 19
    of whaling ships, 24-25, 27
Clarke, Edward, 82
Coast Survey
    and Maria Mitchell's discovery of
        comet, 46
    Maria Mitchell's work for, 50-51
    William Mitchell's work for, 22,
        24-25
Collegio Romano, Observatory of,
    64-65
Columbia University, honorary LL.D.
    from, 50
Comet, Mitchell's discovery of, 44-50
Cornell University, 84
Crosby, Alphonsus, 70-71

Darwin, Charles, 41
Davis, Charles Henry, 50
Deep South, Mitchell in, 57
Denmark, King of, gold medal from,
    46-49
Denver, and solar eclipse, 12-19, 76
Dickens, Charles, 34
Dickinson, Anna, 89
Dix, Dorothea, 53

Edison, Thomas Alva, 16
Emerson, Ralph Waldo, 35, 59
England, Mitchell in, 59-62, 83
Ephemeris, 50, 54, 67, 70
Europe, Mitchell's travels in, 54,
    58-66, 83
Everett, Edward, 48-49, 59

Folger, Phoebe, 24
Folger, Walter, 24

Galileo, 65
Gauss, Karl Friedrich, 33

Index

Germany, Mitchell in, 65-66, 83

Girton College, 83

Gold medal, for comet discovery, 46-49

Gravitation (Airy), 33

Greeley, Horace, 35, 36-37

Greenwich Observatory, 59

Harvard College, 84, 85
    Annex, 85
    Observatory, 31, 32, 46, 49
    Radcliffe, 85

Hawthorne, Nathaniel, 62-64

Henry, Joseph, 59

Herschel, Caroline, 60, 82

Herschel, John, 59-60

Herschel, William, 59-60

Howe, Julia Ward, 23, 77, 89, 90

Humboldt, Alexander von, 65-66

Italy, Mitchell in, 62-65

Jupiter, 99

Ladd-Franklin, Christine, 98

Leverrier, Urbain, 62

Livermore, Mary, 89, 90

Liverpool Observatory, 59

London, Mitchell in, 59-62

Lyceum lectures, 35-37

Maria Mitchell Association of Nantucket, 99

Maria Mitchell Women in Science Award, 99

Melville, Herman, 35

Mississippi River, Mitchell's trip down, 56-57

Mitchell, Andrew (brother), 22, 39, 42

Mitchell, Anne (sister), 22, 42

Mitchell, Forster (brother), 22

Mitchell, Henry (brother), 22, 25, 27, 33, 42

Mitchell, Kate (sister), 22, 23, 42, 67, 96

Mitchell, Lydia (mother), 22, 24, 66-67

Mitchell, Maria
    and astronomical work with father, 25-27, 31-32, 43, 45-46, 48, 51, 67
    birth of, 20
    character of, 19
    childhood of, 20-27
    and Coast Survey, 50-51
    as computer for almanac, 50, 54, 67, 70
    and critical capacity, 33, 35-37
    and daily schedule, 30-31
    death of, 94-95, 97
    and discovery of comet, 44-50
    and early experience with astronomy, 12, 26-27, 31-32, 43
    and early love of astronomy, 19, 25, 26-27, 32
    education of, 24, 25, 32-37
    and 1831 solar eclipse, 19, 27
    and 1878 solar eclipse, 12-19, 76
    family of, 21-27, 40-43, 66-67. *See also* Mitchell, William
    and funeral, 79, 97
    generosity of, 38
    and home life and personal interests, 51-53
    and honors and awards, 46-50
    and ill health, 96-97
    and lecturing, 77, 82, 87, 88-89
    legacy of, 97-99
    as librarian, 30, 38, 43, 51, 54, 80-81
    and new telescope, 67
    as professor. *See* Vassar Female College
    and publications, 51, 77, 82, 99
    and Quakers, 21-22, 38-41
    and religious beliefs, 38-41
    and school on Nantucket, 28-30
    as self-supporting, 28

Index

and sense of humor, 37-38
and travels in Europe, 54, 58-66, 83
and travels in U.S., 55-57, 84-85
as unconventional, 38
as Unitarian, 40, 92-95
See also Women's rights
Mitchell, Peleg (uncle), 41
Mitchell, Phebe (sister), 17, 22, 38,
42, 64
Mitchell, Polly (niece), 42
Mitchell, Sally (sister), 22, 42
Mitchell, William (father), 23, 24
as bank cashier, 24, 27
and Coast Survey, 24-25, 32
death of, 79
and devotion to astronomy, 24-25,
26-27, 31-32, 43
and 1831 solar eclipse, 19
and Harvard College, 48
with Maria at Vassar, 71, 74, 77,
79, 85
Maria's astronomical work with,
25-27, 31-32, 43, 45-46, 48,
51, 67
and Maria's comet discovery,
45-46, 48
and Nantucket Philosophical
Society, 34-35
and Quakers, 21-22, 41
school of, 25, 30
Mitchell, William Forster (brother),
22, 42

Nantucket
and fire of 1846, 43
and Maria Mitchell Association of
Nantucket, 99
Mitchell's childhood on, 20-27
and Mitchell's early astronomy
on, 26-27, 31-32
Mitchell's school on, 28-30
Mitchell vacationing in, 96
Quakers of, 21-22, 38-41

Nantucket Atheneum
and fire of 1846, 43
and Mitchell as librarian, 30, 38,
43, 51, 80-81
and Mitchell's education, 33-37
Mitchell's resignation from, 54
Nantucket Philosophical Society, 24,
34-35
National Women Suffrage
Association, 90
Nautical Almanac, 67, 70
"Need of Women in Science, The," 91
*New American Practical Navigator,
The* (Bowditch), 33
New Orleans, Mitchell in, 57

"Observations on Some of the
Double Stars," 51

Pacific Bank, 24, 27, 32, 43, 44, 67
Paris, Mitchell in, 62
Parker, Theodore, 35
Peirce, Benjamin, 70
Peirce, Reverend Cyrus, 25

Quakers, 21-22, 38
and Mitchell family, 21-22, 40-42
Mitchell leaving, 38-41
Quincy, Josiah Jr., 35-36

Raymond, J.H., 85, 92
Richards, Ellen Swallow, 98
Rome, Mitchell in, 63, 64
Russia, Mitchell in, 83
Rutgers Female College, honorary
Ph.D. from, 50

Saturn, 99
Schumaker, Christian, 49
Secchi, Father, 64-65
Sex in Education (Clarke), 82
Slavery, 41, 57
Smith, Elizabeth Oakes, 35

Index

Smithsonian Institution, 49
Smith College, 84-85
Social Reading Society, 35
Solar eclipse
    of 1831, 19, 27
    of 1878, 12-19, 76
    partial, 15
Somerville, Mary, 64, 65
Stanton, Elizabeth Cady, 89, 90
Stone, Lucy, 35
Sunspots, 99
Swarthmore College, 85
Swift, H.K., 56-57
Swift, Prudence, 55-62
Switzerland, Mitchell in, 83

Taylor, James Monroe, 94, 96, 97
Telescopes
    for 1878 eclipse, 13, 14, 16, 18, 19
    as gift to Mitchell, 67
    and Mitchell's comet discovery,
        44-45
    repairs on, 32
    at Vassar, 72-73
Thoreau, Henry David, 35

Unitarianism, 40, 92-95
Uranus, 60

Vassar, Matthew, 68, 69-70, 71, 92
Vassar, Matthew Jr., 87
Vassar Female College, 12-13, 68-70
    and attempts to oust Mitchell on
        religious grounds, 92-94
    and "dome parties," 77
    financial difficulties at, 87-90
    founding of, 68-70
    and Mitchell as fundraiser, 87,
        95, 97
    and Mitchell as Unitarian, 92-95
    Mitchell's appointment to, 70-71

and Mitchell's "effort to grasp
    great truths," 74-77
and Mitchell's effort to liberate
    students, 77-79
Mitchell's father at, 71, 74, 77,
    79, 85
and Mitchell's fight for women's
    rights, 82-83, 85-86, 87-88, 92
Mitchell's legacy to, 97-99
and Mitchell's resignation, 97
and Mitchell's salary, 71, 85-86
and Mitchell's students on trip to
    solar eclipse, 12-19, 76
observatory at, 71-73, 77, 87,
    95-96, 97
and Whitney as assistant, 96, 97
Vatican, observatory in, 64-65
Venus, 50
Von Struve, Frederick G.W., 59

Whaling ships, chronometers of,
    24-25, 27
Whewell, William, 59
Whitman, Walt, 35
Whitney, Mary, 96, 97, 98
Widow's walk, 26
Women's rights, 80-91, 95
    and Association for the Advance-
        ment of Women, 90-91
    and education, 80-85, 87
    and friends involved in, 89-90
    and lyceum talks, 88-89
    and Mitchell's legacy, 98, 99
    and Mitchell's trip to Europe, 83
    and political action meetings, 89
    at Vassar, 82-83, 85-86
    and women on faculties and
        boards of trustees of college,
        87-88
Wood, Frances A., 82

Picture Credits

About the Author

DALE ANDERSON studied history and literature at Harvard University. He has worked in publishing ever since. He lives with his wife and two sons in Newtown, Pennsylvania, where he writes and edits textbooks and reference books. He has written several books for young adults, including *Westward Expansion, The Cold War Years,* and *America into a New Millennium.*

JILL SIDEMAN, PH.D. serves as vice president of CH2M HILL, an international environmental-consulting firm based in San Francisco. She was among the few women to study physical chemistry and quantum mechanics in the late 1960s and conducted over seven years of post-doctoral research in high-energy physics and molecular biology. In 1974, she co-founded a woman-owned environmental-consulting firm that became a major force in environmental-impact analysis, wetlands and coastal zone management, and energy conservation. She went on to become Director of Environmental Planning and Senior Client Service Manager at CH2M HILL. An active advocate of women in the sciences, she was elected in 2001 as president of the Association for Women in Science, a national organization "dedicated to achieving equity and full participation for women in science, mathematics, engineering and technology."